WALKING IN THE
PROPHETIC ANOINTING

WALKING IN THE PROPHETIC ANOINTING

Requires Knowing Your Calling, Listening to God's Voice, and Enduring the Test

LATOYA HEWITT PANTON

Palmetto Publishing Group
Charleston, SC

Walking in the Prophetic Anointing
Copyright © 2020 by Latoya Hewitt Panton
All rights reserved

First Edition

Printed in the United States

ISBN-13: 978-1-64990-171-2
ISBN-10: 1-64990-171-2

Let me start by saying thanks to the eternal, immortal, and all-knowing God for his divine inspiration in writing this book. I also want to thank my mother, Zichar Morrison, for her constant prayers and encouragement. Next I want to recognize my wonderful and supportive husband, Ernesto Panton, and children, Jago and Daniel Panton, who have stood with me every step of the way. Last but not least, I want to say thank you to Miss Campbell (New Day All Age School), Miss Edwards (my ELA teacher), Mr. Ennis (my Engineering teacher), and all the teachers from the Kingston Technical High School (1994-1998) who contributed to my success.

I dedicate this book to the memory of my loving grandmother, Cardell Palmer, a true warrior.

When the storm passes, and the thunder roars no more, when the clouds vanish forever from the sky, we will be safe in the hands of the perpetual God whose mystery lies in the hidden foundation of the heavens and the earth.

—Latoya Panton

Nothing gives me more pleasure than to inspire, motivate, and uplift others. With the motivation of the Holy Spirit, I have written this book in hope of encouraging and strengthening someone who may have encountered battle after battle in life and at times may have felt like quitting was the only option. Whether you are charting unfamiliar waters, or you are challenged by life circumstances, I encourage you to embrace your storms, because God is your anchor. May each page of this book strengthen your heart and provide you with additional insights to fight your Goliaths as you walk in your calling.

CONTENTS

INTRODUCTION

Isn't it interesting how God puts us in unfamiliar situations that sometimes seem nonsensical and uncomfortable? It is like telling a student who is a pro at playing basketball that he needs to get his grades up if he plans to continue playing on the team. When all he knows is that he is the best jump shooter there is. Furthermore he has the most reliable three-point shot on any given day. What is even more amazing is how we as parents put our children in activities that in some ways are so rigorous and painstakingly difficult that we ourselves would not even have the guts to attempt, much less succeed at, but we expect our children to do it with little challenge. These activities could range from preparing for the spelling bee championship, a tennis game, or swimming tournaments. In our minds we are preparing them to take on life challenges and to acquire certain traits such as discipline, resilience, and tenacity. All of which will help to cultivate them into becoming a successful person; only "they" don't know it yet!

I remember taking my younger son, Daniel, to swimming lessons for the first time. I thought that with him being a good soccer player, he would not have much difficulty in learning a new skill such as swimming. So on the first day of class, his brother and I were overwhelmingly excited, and he also seemed to be a little anxious to learn swimming. However, as he began his water acclimation lessons, he became scared and frightened. Later as the coach began to carry him out further into the water, Daniel became more and more terrified. His eyes seemed to become enlarged, and his stomach blew up like a giant volcano ready to erupt. I can recall shouting from across the room, "You got this, Daniel!"

He would glance at me momentarily as if to say, "Mom, why are you allowing this guy to kill me?" While sitting on the chair in the pool room, I thought, "He is younger than I am, so this should not be that difficult for him." After the first lesson, his body language echoed, "I do not want to come back here!"

In an attempt to capture his feelings about what had just happened,

I asked, "So, Daniel, how do you feel about your first class?"

With a sharp turn and a look of bewilderment, he gazed at me and said, "Mom, can I do something else? I don't want to learn to swim anymore!"

"No way!" I thought. "Is this the same Daniel that was so excited about swimming lessons and literally begging me weeks earlier to take him to swimming classes?" Though his response was surprising, I could understand how he felt about the whole ordeal. You see, while playing soccer allowed him to have direct contact with the ground, swimming did not. While he was able to use his foot skills to control the ball in soccer, he did not have that leverage in swimming. This new aquatic exploration required him to become almost totally dependent on an unseen force to keep him balanced and glide in the water along with his ability to navigate it with his hands and legs. Swimming required him to give some amount of control to the water, which made it scary. In science we learn that light things float and heavy objects sink. We sometimes carry out experiments on these different objects to see how they react when in the water. A feather, for example, when placed in the water will just begin floating. However, a stone or pebble once placed in the water will automatically sink to the bottom. According to *Archimedes's law*, any body completely or partially submerged in a fluid (gas or liquid) at rest is acted upon by an upward, or buoyant, force, the magnitude of which is equal to the weight of the fluid displaced by the body.

In the coming months, Daniel would begin to have a change in his attitude. He realized that once he learned to control his breathing, float, and coordinate his body movements, he became more and more confident, and he was better able to navigate his way through the water.

Like Daniel and so many others, I had to learn the same lessons. Being in an unfamiliar situation, though tough, I was going to survive. With God's Word and guidance, I would be able to overcome my giants and my fears. I was going to be able to learn new survival skills and grow in knowledge and wisdom as a person. As a result, I could live victoriously over sin, and negative energy. Furthermore, I would be able to impact others around me in a positive way. Through knowledge and revelation of the Word of God, I would be able to use the tools that God had given me to overcome even the harshest circumstances. Subsequently, I would be able to apply the knowledge and skills that I had learned in past situations to overcome my current battles or struggles in life. Like Daniel, I had a coach; the only difference was that Daniel could see his coach in person and was able to communicate with him face-to-face. Additionally, Daniel was also able to receive real-time feedback from his coach, who held his hand and provided emotional support as he acclimatized to his new environment. On the contrary, many times the only real-time feedback I had from God was my faith and trust in his words. I had to trust God's hand when I could not see his face and trust his grace to carry me safely through troubled times. The Word of God provided the cushion I needed as I navigated life uncertainties. I have set the Lord always before me; because he is at my right hand, I shall not be moved (Psalms 16:8). Hence I now understand that God's intention for my life exceeded what I could ever have asked or imagined.

AFFIRMATIONS

When I am weak, he is strong.
When I am in doubt, he is most certain.
When I am clueless, he is all knowing.
When I am powerless, he is all powerful.
----Latoya Hewitt Panton

CHAPTER 1

Trusting God in Unfamiliar Places

*Your eyes saw my substance, being yet unformed. And in Your book they all were written, The days fashioned for me, When **as yet there were** none of them.*
—Psalms 139:16

This was just one of the main verses from the good book that resonated in my spirits as I faced life uncertainties. Ever had your entire dream of what you hoped you would become totally transformed, and everything you thought you knew metamorphose into what seems like a big bang? Well, welcome to hearing the voice of God.

Hearing God's voice and walking in the prophetic word would later form the epicenter of what was to come in my life. Having sought the Lord diligently, and received the prophetic confirmation to accept a teaching opportunity over distant land, I later braced myself for what was to come. Overcome with joy and amazement at what God was doing in my life, I tried to make sense of it all: "what was to become my new normal." I was about to leave the known for the unknown—my spouse, my young children, my parents, and every sense of my normal existence for the opportunity that would bring my family and I a better life. Though this experience would carry me over distant waters, it was not the first of its kind. I remembered many times in the past when I commuted by bus to work, that I would hear the voice of God telling me to preach the word. Sometimes I would become so defiant, and resisted the voice of God until his Presence would overwhelm me so much that I had to submit to his will and started preaching the gospel. At other times I would be at my local church and hear the voice of the Lord telling me to speak. As usual I would become reluctant until the words just began to burst out of my mouth. Hence, I knew that the power of the Spirit of God was stronger than anything I could ever experienced. As the days drew closer, I would be embraced and reminded by witnesses of the prophecy pronounced over my destiny weeks earlier. Some would say, "So when are you leaving?"

READER NOTE

Throughout each of the chapters in this book there are reflections, and activities. These sections serve to help you engage with key ideas in the chapter. Reflections can be a good way of examining ourselves, our perspective, and actions. It provides valuable insights as we move forward in our spiritual walk with God.

"Can I çome with you?" echoed another. This provided a constant reminder of what God was about to do in my life. The mission and purpose for which I was endowed had settled deep in my spirit as I surrendered my will to Him.

PREPARING FOR TAKE OFF

After months of preparing myself mentally, the day had come for me to board my flight to distant shores. I remembered leisurely pulling myself out of bed that morning, trying to secure the scenery of where I had called home for two years. I relished the taste of ackee and saltfish with roast breadfruit that my mother had prepared some hours earlier and the sweet smelling savor of the fresh mint tea that caressed my nostrils as I drank from the cup. My husband, though in a somber mood, was meticulously policing my luggage to ensure that it was aligned with the travel guidelines. It was one of the qualities that I had come to appreciate about him over the years. He was the earthly lieutenant of my life, Gently though firmly guiding me on my journey to success. My older son, Jago, was the mini version of his dad: strong, calm, and secured. He would at times envelope his arms around my neck, which left me feeling like a mother eagle who had to go hunt to find some delightful meal to soothe the soul of her little eaglet. The sun had barely peeked out of the sky when we embarked on our journey to the Norman Manley International airport to which I had traveled five years prior. The feeling of uncertainty came rushing back to that familiar spot. The memories quickly paused as my thoughts flashed to the scenes of my kinsmen along the roadside, selling their wares and conversing. My mind suddenly joined the conversation of the two men standing on the sidewalk adjacent to a grocery store, exchanging pleasantries. They hugged and bumped fist as their laughter catapulted into the atmosphere. The synergy between them showed a rich, organic friendship from the past, or maybe long-lost relatives that had somehow reunited. But whatever the case, their unity reminded me of who we were as a people. At the core of our spirit, we were warm and compassionate, always carrying in our spirit a care for each other, though at times we seemed foreign. However, whenever the moment of victory arose, our spirits, like a host of angels, would unite, and with one big chorus we would sing each other's praises. With the airport in sight, I quickly collected my thoughts and prepared my belongings to exit the vehicle. As we walked through the airport, we saw many passengers coming in and many others leaving; there was a constant movement of both people and planes. After checking in and receiving my boarding pass, my husband and I sat once more for what would be our last face-to-face conversation for months to come. Our faith in God made all the difference; we had been prepared and were ready to embark on this new phase in our lives. As I parted to board my flight, I felt assured and hopeful of the future as I embarked on the new journey ahead.

REFLECTION

Whether it is to enlist in the army, to travel over distant waters in search of a new opportunity, or because of a divorce. People make the heart wrenching decision to leave their families everyday. Have you ever had to leave your family? What was this experience like for you?

THE JOURNEY

In retrospect, my journey to success did not begin when I received the prophetic word, but in fact, it began from my very existence. I remembered my mother telling me how she cried to God to take me for the entire nine months that she carried me in her womb. In her words, "I did not know God, and I was told by everyone that I was going to suffer with you, so like Hannah I prayed that God would take you."

As life unfolded her words would come to have great relevance in my life. Two decades later, after walking through many hills and valleys, I would come to realize that where my husband and I started, "his hometown," was only a rest stop that was not meant to be permanent. Furthermore, it was at this "rest stop" that God's plan and his glory for my life would begin to unfold. It's funny how often when we find ourselves in an uncomfortable, or unfamiliar situation, we are unable to connect the past experiences we have had with our present situation. This may be due sometimes to the harsh and unbearable circumstances we find ourselves in. It would take several years for me to unravel the mystery of how God was going to reshape my mindset, attitudes, and beliefs to come in alignment with his plan and purpose for my life. "Ever heard the saying, I escaped like a bird in the night?" Well, that was me. The way that God would deliver me out of my Marah experience mirrored how God took the Israelites out of the hands of the Egyptians. In the book of Exodus, we saw where the Lord had heard the cry of the people of Israel and had sent Moses, to deliver them out of the bondage they were in. I felt like the people of Israel in many instances. I knew that there was a God—I read about him in the good book, but I could not fathom how he was going to deliver me out of my Egypt situation. I had settled in the hometown of an unknown people, an unknown social construct in the hope that my family could have had a better start. Instead I was to encounter what seemed to be a generational stronghold, a regime laced with hate, discrimination, and ideological and systematic oppression, and suppression. I had often read in the scriptures where God would remind his people that when they walked through the flood, they would not drown, and when they walked through the fire, it would not burn them. It was in this unfamiliar place that I realized that I was not just reading the words of the scriptures, but I was also living the word.

DAIRY OF THE DESSERT EXPERIENCE

It was a new day, a new season, and a new life. I had found myself in a social dynasty, a way of life, a social phenomenon: the "ghetto." The ghetto, as it was called, was where I would experience the crushing of the flesh, and the dying of self in the backside of the desert. Furthermore, I would understand more about the principle of love and forgiveness, and receive a deeper revelation of God's call on my life. I would learn that humility is not thinking less of yourself, it's thinking of yourself less (C.S. Lewis). Forgiveness was not independent of love; in fact it was the very core of love. For you to truly forgive your enemies or those that hurt you, you must first love them. So love is not just an act, but it is a way of life. To many the ghetto, or the "hood," is a slum, a place often riddled by the bullets of turf wars and poverty. The place where tension is often fueled by oppression, and the hardship among close friends, family members, and neighboring communities. A place where many embattled souls hustled to survive. At first glance, it seemed like any normal low-income community, with white-washed walls that seemed to camouflage the true hardship of its times; the rustic buildings that seemed to whisper the pitch-black hardship of ancestors that traveled before and faces of embattled warriors who had escaped the fist of death stood securely in their positions like great men and women who made it to the hallmark of fame. The ghetto meant different things to different people. For many the ghetto offered them hope, a means to an end. It was a place where you could start your life with whatever little resources you had and you did not have to face the harsh criticism from others because of your inability to live up to a certain standard of living. For some like me, the ghetto was a place where dreams could become a reality. Being in the ghetto I joined in the hustle to achieve my goals and aspirations. Whether it was to build a dream house, buy a car, or send your children to college—living in the ghetto made it possible. The ghetto was like a refuge center for many who were not born with a "golden spoon" in their mouths but needed to begin life with the little resources they had. In essence the ghetto could be whatever you wanted it to be. Being in the ghetto, I would see and hear of many lives snuffed out by the gun, and I saw the pain and anguish of many families torn by the loss of a loved one. I can recall my first experience of the tragedy that struck the community. It was like the bombing of Pearl Harbor by the Japanese, no one expected it. One of the neighbors, whom I will refer to as Joe, had heard the crippling news that his son had been shot by gun men some distance away. Like wildfire the news spread throughout the community and within seconds there was a massive gathering in the streets. The sound of sirens echoed freely over houses and tree tops. The sting of death had strike once again. It was as though darkness had climbed to its highest peak and the ocean cried a sea of tears. Mothers wept, and fathers stood helplessly in the distant, clutching their faces in dismay as they tried to mentally connect the missing pieces to the puzzle. The sorrow was uncontrollable and understandably so. Joe had lost his only son, his prince and the heir to his dynasty. No one saw this coming; no one had a clue. But one thing was for sure: his death would not go in vain. Whoever was to pay would pay, and that was that. This was the start of a whirlwind of battle that would claim the lives of many. In my mind I was certain of one thing—"survival." I was not born to this world in defeat, nor does failure run through my veins. I was not a gazelle waiting to be trampled upon by its prey. I was a lioness with spiritual muscles as sharp as razors. My diet did not consist of the freshly killed corpse of the wilder-beast, a suntanned gazelle or a Savanna-grown giraffe; instead it was loaded with the spiritual arrows, and missiles of the Word of God. Hence, defeat was not an option.

MAINTAINING FOCUS IN THE DESERT

Being in the "ghetto," provided new challenges that required me to stay mentally alert. The senseless quarrels from the neighbors, and the frequent tensions between nearby communities, were a constant reminder that I could not become comfortable. Many days as I peruse my new environment, I notice that though milk and honey were present, there were many giants in the land. However, I affirmed myself in the Word of God, and remained positive. My circumstances would soon become my motivation, my inspiration; my mountain to climb. With each and every passing day, I would revisit my daily expectations and future goals. I self-talked and dreamed, and I wrote my daily affirmations that would keep me steadily on the path to success. As I pressed toward the light, the giants would begin to glare their ugly heads. But like a lion refusing to be trapped in defeat, I would later rise to the occasion and fight strategically with every spiritual fiber in my body.

EMPLOYING SPIRITUAL TOOLS IN THE BACKSIDE OF THE DESERT

Being isolated does not mean that you are a lone; rather it means that you are divinely set apart and positioned for greatness.
---Latoya Hewitt Panton

My experience of the backside of the desert was like being in a cesspool of hate and rejection. The physical environment embodied that of the spiritual struggle and oppression that was the undercurrent that ran deep within the community. The debris, and the foul smell from the water that ran loosely from the waste pipes were a constant reminder that I could not remain comfortable in my present condition. I felt like an ant caught in the trap of a spider. The only tool of defense I had was my ability to hear God's voice and to offer up sacrifices of praise to him that would later become my spiritual therapy. Praise not only offered me a way of escape from the chaos, but it provided the daily spiritual nourishment my soul needed to stay in tune with God.

REFLECTION

Think about a time when you were placed in a desert situation. How did it help to reshape your life?

FIGHTING PHYSICAL GIANTS SPIRITUALLY

Though we walk in the flesh we do not wrestle
against the flesh but against the spirit
—2 Corinthians 10:3

The Word of God would help me to fight against the daily hurling of insults, and negativity that oozed from the outside forces. There were just a handful of people who had made themselves as weapons of darkness to fight against any measure of success I tried to pursue. I could not understand why one would have a problem with someone wanting to be successful, someone wanting to be of relevance to society, someone wanting to become the best version of themselve. I soon discovered that it was not just about me wanting to

be successful, but it was what it represented in my generation and those that came after me. It was the fear that crippled so many who did not understand the movement of God.
Moreover, it was as a result of the call of God on my life. I
remembered having traveled to North Carolina to complete
my first degree and finding myself at a Baptist church in the
community. With no time to unravel the circumstances that
led me to the church, I found myself ministering to the Sunday
school superintendent, and delivering God's Word to her. You
see, God was getting ready to do a new thing, and she needed
to be aligned with what God was doing. I remembered step-
ping into the Sunday school and seeing the young people walking into the room. Immediately the Presence of God fell in that
place. The way that the Glory of God rested in the atmosphere
reminded me of the pillar of cloud that stood at the door of
the tabernacle when God spoke to Moses (Exodus33:9). Upon
being led by the Holy Spirit I delivered the Word of the God to
her, and before I was finished ministering to her she was rolling
uncontrollably on the ground. Though frightened I rose up in
the power of the Holy Spirit and began to anoint her as the
Spirit of God led me. Later, the Holy Spirit was to continue
with a spate of manifestation that left me spiritually intoxicat-
ed. This opened another chapter of the working of the Holy
Spirit, and the power of God. I remembered while traveling
back from the mission of the Lord, his still small voice spoke
to me in my room. His exact words were, "I have silenced all
your enemies." Upon my return to the back side of the dessert, I would notice that some of my enemies had disappeared,

and some seemed a little more controlled. However, He would continue to break me, and rid me of all worldly desire. There my desire for the things of God would begin to strengthen. With that realization I pressed toward the mark of the high calling in Christ Jesus.

REFLECTION

For many, experiencing the outpouring of the Spirit of God can be overwhelming. How would you describe your time in the Presence of God?

ACTIVITY
STOP-AND-THINK

Having experienced the spiritual move of God, some people talk of experiencing a "spiritual crash," after going back home to their regular routine.

1. Have you experienced this, "spiritual crash?"
2. What are two things that you can do to avoid the spiritual crash?

CHAPTER 2

ENDURING THE CRUSH

Seeking God in my unfamiliar place would continue to be my number one priority. In the words of Frank Herbert, "Survival is the ability to swim in strange water." Countless times I would have to grapple with the feeling of belonging, the feeling of hate, the feeling of doubt. Was I sure I had heard from God? Why would He have told me to settle in a place where I would be hated, rejected, ostracized, and ridiculed? I reasoned within myself as I endured the daily hammering of insults from my haters. Their ugly words would press against the core of my spirit daily. Have you ever thought of changing yourself, or adjusting your beliefs to fit in? Well that was me. In trying to be at peace with myself, I thought the only way out was to change me. In Jean Piaget study, (as cited by Carpendale, and Müller,2003), "The need to belong to a particular society is one of the essential parts of human nature." Understanding that changing myself to feel a sense of belonging was not what God had designed for me, I pressed on. I pressed through daily insults of "You don't belong here; you need to go back to where you came from!" In years to come, I would learn to lean on God and trust his word when I could not see his face, and I leaned on his grace to carry me through difficult times. But how would this situation have impacted me spiritually? Throughout this time I would learn the art of pressing through the crushing. I would give way to the humiliation, the daily dying of self. Sometimes, in silence; at other times I would just become so aggravated and lash out verbally at my haters. Then I would realize that I was still in the embryonic stage of understanding the call of God and the ministry set before me. I had not fully learned to let go and allow God to fight my battles. Many similar episodes would unfold before I realized that God did not need me to help him fight the battle. So I delved deeper into God's Word and asked him daily to help me to understand his vision for my life. While doing this I had to develop the tenacity of a lion and the ferociousness of a bulldog to override the daily negativity that seemed to ooze from the tongues of the enemy like angry flames from a wooden fire. As the outside voices threw their criticisms and hate at my marriage, my profession, and my life, I pushed back with the Word of God. "I can do all things through Christ who strengthens me" (Philippians 4:13) and "God is a present help in the time of trouble, therefore I will not fear though the earth be removed and though the mountains be carried into the midst of the sea" (Psalms 46:1). It was then that I would notice my enemies subdued into silence. Learning to trust God in difficult places would take me nine and a half years. However, I was going to learn what God wanted me to learn, and I was going to learn it quickly.

REFLECTION

On our spiritual walk with God, he tends to put us in crushing situations. These situations though uncomfortable are not meant to crush us, instead they are meant to make us stronger. What was one thing you learned about yourself while going through the "CRUSH?"

DIVINELY POSITIONED

While in the "ghetto," I saw many others that had made the journey before me. Some were on that same spiritual training ground to produce the fruit of the Spirit that they needed for their ministry to which God had called them, while others were just seeking an opportunity for a better life. In some ways I believe that I was divinely tricked because in my mind I was only there for the opportunity of a better start financially, only to find out that I was being trained to fight spiritual battles and to die to self daily. My spiritual confidants would often try to comfort me by sharing their experiences of the struggle they faced. Some told me not to worry about what others wanted to say. However, they were well advanced in years, so in my mind, "it was easier said than done." In my head this was the worst experience I could have ever gone through. Here I am a young Christian disciple of Jesus Christ who had faithfully sought God and trusted him with my future goals and aspirations, only to find myself being hated, disgraced, and hammered for being ambitious, hardworking, and relentless in my pursuit for excellence. Ridiculed for adapting the principles of the Word of God; hated for choosing to educate myself to fight the ignorance of society, and trampled upon for my very existence. Trying to make sense of my situation would only end in a whirlwind of confusion. However, God knew that it would take all this and more to get rid of my naivety, and self-pity.

MEETING IN THE SECRET PLACE

I daily looked for God in our secret meeting place, a place where I would pour out of my spirit all the hate, discomfort, and torment I felt. Then within the stillness of the moment, he would remind me that he existed before the world began; he created the light and the darkness. As a result, he could create light within the darkness. He could also tell the light when to come out and the darkness where to hide. Soon I would secure my mind around the thought that, "if he could set the boundaries of the sea, then he could set the boundaries for the enemy as well." I also realized that the enemy was the controlled variable in my life. Their growth and power depended on how much I fed them. The independent variable was the love of God for me and his purpose that could not be aborted. The truth is I had been divinely positioned by God, only I did not recognize the share ingenuity of God's plans.

USING WHAT YOU KNOW

In education the term "schema" is used to define the way in which children and adults process information. In Winn study, (as cited by Neumann and Kopcha ,2018), "A schema is an abstract representation; it is a dynamic structure that provides context for new learning and interpretation that can be modified by instruction and experience." Hence I had to rely on my schema of how God had made all things work together for good to them that love him and are called according to his purpose (Romans 8:28). This would deepen my understanding of what was to come in the future.

CONFRONTING YOUR GOLIATH

The story is told in the Bible of David and Goliath. David used his knowledge of God's ability to deliver him countless times when he was attacked by the bears and the lions to know that God was able to physically, mentally, and spiritually deliver him for all other circumstances. By relying on God's strength, David would gain the spiritual fortitude to overcome one of the biggest challenges of his life—his Goliath. I soon realized that if I was going to overcome my Goliath, I had to trust my previous experiences of God and how he had brought me out of difficult situations. As the days rolled on, I reflected on my days in college when the stress of college life became burdensome. It was only my faith in God that kept me a midst the challenging times. I remember having to sit several exams one semester, and thinking to myself, "how on earth was I going to overcome this task?" For one particular course for which I had been studying for weeks, I had literally spoken to every bird of the air, every beast of the field, and every element in the atmosphere about the content of this course in an attempt to solidify it in my brain. However, on the day of the exam, I was so drained that I could not remember the majority of what I had studied. Finding myself on the day of the exam feeling bewildered and exhausted, I decided to pray and trust God to pull me through. After sitting the exam and realizing I had overcome the worst, my trust in God solidified once again. I took solace in the fact that, "He who has begun a good work in you will complete it until the day of Jesus Christ (Philippians 1:6).

REFLECTION

Though our battles may be different we all go through different struggles in our lives. What was one struggle that you thought was the most challenging? What tools did you employ to help you overcome the challenge?

BIRTHING THE VICTORY THROUGH PAIN

The birthing of my two boys still remains one of the most life-changing and memorable experiences I have ever had. I can still remember my two deliveries like they were yesterday. After I had gone through the morning sickness, discomfort, and fatigue for thirty-nine weeks, the time had come for me to give birth to my firstborn boy, "Jago." I had checked into the hospital on doctor's orders and had processed my paperwork. Before I knew it, I was in the delivery ward, with pains moving up and down my spine like a garden rake pulling and scraping at every turn. With my husband in sight, I felt I was not alone. However, the constant trigger of the pain up and down my spine was a constant reminder that even though I had the support of my family, I was going to have to go through the physical process of this delivery on my own. Gathering strength from the nurses and midwives that stood by my bedside, I responded to every instruction given to me for when to push and when to refrain from pushing. I became totally submissive to the nurses and midwives and had no doubt in their ability to guide me through this process. As the pains of labor rocked my body, I would sometimes scream and holler, hoping to get some relief from any spiritual source. My grandmother, or my mother; the ancestors, or anybody. It didn't matter. I just needed to be delivered from this agony and petrifying feeling that was wreaking havoc in my body. As the gaps between my contractions grew shorter, and each contraction steadily opened the birth canal, I realized that my miracle was on the horizon. Like I was giving birth, I was aware that while going through my "Marah" experience that God was going to deliver me. If I could follow his instructions, then the purpose would override the pain. Though I would sometimes feel resentful, hateful, worrisome, fearful, and lonely, I was always sure of one thing: "God's Faithfulness." He was always there, walking me through the process and leading me to a greater place in him. How was I to have fathomed that I was birthing a spirit of excellence, a spirit of resilience, a spirit of tenacity, and a spirit of hope. A spirit that would never quit despite the obstacles that presented itself. During my time of spiritual warfare, I focused on the bigger picture, my goals, my dreams, and my aspirations. That meant managing my forty-hour work week, coming home to a young four-year-old asthmatic son, and studying part-time. I learned in that moment that anything that was going to make an impact would come at a high price.

When going through my dessert experience, I learned to pull on the strength and mental fortitude of my past experiences. There were many times that I felt that I was in the wrong place, because God would always put me in an environment where I would have to be isolated, ostracized and rejected. But this was only to protect and perfect his purpose for my life. Later on I realized that I needed to be isolated and experience rejection in order to be fully plunged into my true destiny. Finally, I would learn the valuable lesson of "how to not try to fit in, and how to stand in my own spiritual identity." I learned how to trust in my spiritual and cultural heritage of God.

REFLECTION

Human beings are naturally created to socialize, and form relationships. However, at times God will separate us from others to fulfill his plans in our lives. Do you find yourself separated from others most of the time? How has this helped you to fulfill God's purpose for your life?

ACTIVITIES
STOP-AND-THINK

1. Based on your experiences, What is one word that comes to your mind when you think about trusting God?

2. Write True or False to complete the statement below. Your "Desert Experiences," can make you or break you?

   _____

3. Complete the sentence below:
   Experiencing the presence of the Lord is like:

   _____

BRAVERY

She models her stripes like a proud peacock.
Coupled with the tenacity of a lion,
her power is undeniable.
Bravery, she never second-guesses.
She never yields to negativity.
Like a firecracker, she explodes in her heavenly abilities
To face life uncertainty
---Latoya Hewitt Panton

CHAPTER 3

BUILDING ON MY ROUTES

"**Y**ou better make sure that by the time I go down to the house and return, you finish drinking that tea," echoed my grandmother as her short robust figure dashed through the kitchen door.

I can still remember her like it was yesterday. Undoubtedly she was one of the strongest people I knew. She was a natural humanitarian, one who connected with everyone from every walk of life. You did not have to be in her presence for more than ten minutes to know that this was a no-nonsense woman. Whether you were a man or woman, she would be bold to tell you how she felt about whatever topic you were discussing. Curdell Palmer, affectionately called Aunt Cur, was the woman who did not believe in depending on anyone; she worked for what she wanted, and she worked hard.

As a single parent of three girls, she would suffer the harsh reality of her time, which meant struggling alone to care for her children. In some ways she reflected the sentiments of Sojourner Truth: "That man over there says that women need to be helped into carriages, and lifted over ditches, and to have the best place everywhere. Nobody ever helps me into carriages, or over mud-puddles, or gives me any best place! And ain't I a woman?" I would come to know her struggles and see her fight relentlessly for what she holds dare.

In the coming years, I would grow to know her as mom. I still remember her trudging up the narrow hill with me in a small community of Manchester, called Lancaster district. She had left me at the neighbor's house while she went to make her daily game. Working as a domestic helper for one of the more prominent members of the community was her way of life. It was this life that would help to secure her legacy that she would later leave for her children in years to come. It was during one of these days that she would be summoned by the neighbors that her granddaughter had taken an overdose of medication intended for an adult man in his late 80s who had been diagnosed with high blood pressure and many other chronic illnesses. With the memory of what had just happened slowly drifting away, I felt her tightly clutching me over her shoulders. With my body tossing to and fro, she forged ahead with her small feet wrestling with the hilly terrain toward the end of the road. There she would secure a cab to take me to the nearby hospital. I remembered on several occasions she would try to pin my head over her shoulders. However, this proved to be unsuccessful as my head kept swinging back and forth with no sense of stability. Waking up in the hospital, I had no recollection of what happened that afternoon. Instead my attention was focused on the friendly nurse who offered me some scrambled eggs and bread. To me that was one of the most delicious meals I ever had in my life. Later on I saw my biological mother with what seemed to be a worrisome look on her face. Looking back I can imagine the emotional turmoil that she must have gone through to see her four-year-old daughter in that situation. As I reflected on the whole ordeal, it dawned on me that she was the real hero behind us all. Having to work as house help in the town, she would try to generate enough money for my grandmother to take care of the overhead expenses, in the hope that her little girl would be taken care of. Instead, she would later have to face the dis-heartened reality of the tragedy that had unfolded.

REFLECTION

Have you ever had to deal with a crisis situation in your life? How did you cope?

A TRUE DISCIPLINARIAN

As the days rolled on, I would continue to learn more about my grandmother through her many teachings, social inter-actions, and storytelling. She was the kind of woman that would ensure that our Sunday dinner was cooked before going to church. I would sometimes feel a sense of sympathy for my other schoolmates who had to endure that long wait for their Sunday afternoon meal. One of Aunt Cur's strongest features was her discipline techniques. You were to speak the truth and speak it ever, cost it what it will. I remember a time when I had the most brilliant idea. I was to take a little of the sugar from the pan instead of eating the boiled dumplings, green bananas, and salt mackerel (one of Jamaica's finest cuisines) she had prepared. "How was she supposed to have find out?" I thought. I convinced myself that if I had carefully placed the cover on the pan exactly the way it was before, and secured it back in the same exact place, there was no way for her to find out what had happened. But later that day, I realized that what was supposed to be one of my most pleasurable moments turned out to be a catastrophe. My grandmother would soon come back from the shop, and after making her usual spin in the house, she would call me to quarry some matter that might have seemed a bit strange to her. "Nee Nee," shouted my Aunt Cur from the house. "Why you take out the sugar?"

"I didn't trouble the sugar, Aunt Cur!" I hollered from the outside kitchen.

With my Aunt Cur's hallmark discernment, she could detect the lies oozing from my very pulse as I stood there naive as could be. Instead of revealing her findings, she continued to probe me about the sugar, and I continued to convince her that I knew nothing of the matter. It was after she had given me numerous opportunities to confess what I had done that she looked at me pitifully and did not utter another word. Later I had gone to the bushes to play and was stuck in the foot by a "thorn" I came running to Grandma for help. Sure enough she assisted me to take the "thorn" from by foot, but then I felt a firm grip on my blouse. I felt like Brother Cockroach in the Anancy story when Cockroach found himself in Fowl's yard. I knew what was coming next, and sure enough I got a whipping that day that I would not have forgotten anytime soon. From that day on, I learned not to take her lightly. She was never going to allow me to get away with naughty behavior. But how was all this going to shape my attitude and behavior as I grew into a young lady?

REFLECTION

For most of us our grand-parents played an instrumental role in our lives. What is/was one fond memory you have of your grand-parent?

LIFE LESSONS FROM GRANDMA

I remember Aunt Cur going to work miles away from home. Not having a mobile taxi to take us to our destination, we, along with one of Aunt Cur's best friends, Miss Easter, would leave home before the cock crowed. With the stars still fixed in the night sky and the silver giant still offering its magical, magnificent light, we commenced our journey on foot. Many days as we embarked on this journey, I was soon captivated by the huge mansions and immaculate lawns that seemed to whisper melodies of hope and prosperity to me as I walked by. Not to mention the beautiful flowers that elegantly dressed the sides of the road. The beauty of this magnificent sight wiped away any feeling of fatigue and anxiety that would come with this journey. Additionally, the giant hills and tough asphalt stood as a constant reminder of life's challenges. Today when I go back and visit the conception of my childhood years, I am met by taxis and buses that offer their services so readily to take us on these familiar routes where my ancestors and I once joyfully traveled. I grapple with the thought of how we managed to navigate this same journey on foot years prior. I am more than ever convinced that it must have been the grace of God that kept us alive as we sojourn daily over hills and valleys. Like Harriet Tubman, God would light the path for us as we traveled daily. Except; we were never in fear of being caught, nor beaten. This was a time where guns, though birth, were never present and bullets, though formed, were absent. The only thing that came close, was the rattling of the engine of Mr. John's old Ford that seemed to cry of fatigue as it made its way home over monstrous hills. Also not present was the look of hate and envy, pride, or scorn. In the days of my grandmother, I enjoyed the peace and safety that every child of the twenty-first century wished for. I played in the fields, braided the grass, and enjoy going to mango walks with my friends. It was the days when boys played cricket and girls played Dolly House with empty cans, dolls, dirt and leaves. It was the time where neighbors shared lovingly their home, their food, and manual labor for whatever the cause. I remember a time when only one neighbor in our district had a television, and every Sunday afternoon, I would try to hurry and finish my chores so I could go watch the Sunday Matinee with my friends. These were the days of my grandma. I firmly believed that my grandmother's storytelling helped me not to dwell on the challenges of our daily journeys to her job, but instead focus on the positive lessons we could learn from life's challenges. Later, I would learn more about life and its many pitfalls. The high hills and tough pavement would help me to realize that there were many obstacles that I would have to face in life. This experience would later help to shape my character, and mindset into being strong and resilient. My grandmother provided me with real life experiences that would inspire me to become the strong independent woman I am today. I was taught the principle of working for what I wanted and to have hope amid the challenges.

WHEN YOUR FEET HIT THE ROAD

For young children, going to school can provide a wealth of rich experiences that will help to shape their understanding of the world around them.

Attending Frankfield Primary located in the cool parish of Manchester, Lancaster District, did just that for me. My concrete operational years still remain some of the fondest memories I ever had. On a regular school day, I would begin with an early morning bath, a bowl of cornmeal porridge, and freshly ironed uniforms with pleats that seemed to march to the beat of the consciousness that was to follow. As I descended the hills and plateaus that led the lonely route to school, I was greeted with the sun climbing above the trees every morning. As well as the warm heat from the asphalt on the road that slithered through the sole of my ballet shoes. Later the heat would soon cause my shoes to wear out before retiring to their final destination under the cellar in my house. Through these times I would experience many discomforts as my feet would tend to blister on the tough pavement on my way to school. However, this did not stop me from going to school. Like any young child, I had a zeal to learn; I enjoyed the fun moments that school brought. Looking back, I now honor these moments as memorabilia that helped to shape and fashion my future. Had I not had this experience, I would not have known what it meant to fight. I would not have understood what it meant to put your feet firmly on the ground and stand and fight for what I wanted. Growing through these phases of my life taught me to set expectations for myself, and to meet those expectations. I knew what I wanted to become, and I knew that I was going to have to work hard to achieve it. I decided earlier on that I was going to be a lawyer, though I did not have a clue what it meant. I convinced myself upon hearing the term; that it must have meant something good, and that was what I was going to become. Little did I know that God had a different plan.

MAKING AN IMPACT

Making a positive impact, I believe, is one of the strongest contributions one can make to humanity. Whether it is providing food and clothing for the less fortunate, providing clean water for rural communities and poor urban centers throughout the Sub-Saharan Africa, or fighting for the human rights of those who cannot fight for themselves. As human beings we have a responsibility to elevate and uplift those who are oppressed by poverty or life circumstances. Nelson Mandela was by far one of the greatest leaders of our time. Despite his many setbacks as a child and the obstacles he faced as an adult, he stood up for the rights of his fellow countrymen. Though he was later thrown in prison and sentenced to twenty-six years, he did not let his circumstances hinder his mission. Instead, he continued to study and sought to educate other fellow prisoners on their human rights and historical heritage. Later, he was to rise to prominence by becoming one of the greatest black leaders of our time (Broun, 2012). During my time growing up in Jamaica, I would see many aspiring athletes and musicians rise to national greatness. They had one common goal, which was to represent their countrymen and make Jamaica proud. One of my inspirations back then was Merlene Ottey- A true Jamaican patriot. Merlene, who originated from the parish of Hanover, was introduced to the sport of track and field by her mother, who also was a talented runner; she went on to represent Jamaica in seven

Olympic games. Her quest to secure a goal medal at the Olympics was unsuccessful. However, her propensity to always secure a bronze medal earned her the title of the "bronze queen." To many Merlene was far more than just a "bronze queen;" she was our "heroine." What I admire most about her was her resilience and insatiable appetite for winning and for the sport. Though she might never have won a gold medal, her robust determination and shared resilience made her a winner in my eyes. Her last appearance in the 2004 Olympic games came with high expectations for her to secure a goal medal. However, her inability to do so left many of her fans feeling disappointed. In essence, I believe the true lesson to be learned was that "winning does not define who you are; tenacity and will power do." As the saying goes, "The race is not for the swift but for those who can endure to the end." Hence, from that moment on, I understood the desire of wanting to make an impact. Merlene Ottey's passionate spirit penetrated my spirit, and I, too, wanted to make an impact. I not only wanted to make an impact in my family, but I also wanted to make an impact on the wider society, Later on I would discover that the tool kit of education would provide me the opportunity I needed to make a lasting impact on my generation and the world. The humanitarian qualities displayed by my grandmother and my mother also helped to solidify my goal to impact humanity in one way or another. Mother Teresa said it best: "If you can't feed a hundred people, then just feed one."

REFLECTIONS

Most of us in one way or another have made an impact on others. Describe one way in which you were able to make an impact on someone. How did it change your outlook about yourself?

ACTIVITIES
STOP-AND-THINK:

1. Name one person who has inspired you.
2. In what capacity are you called to inspire others?

AFFIRMATIONS

I am not here to wallow in misery and self-pity.
I was not born to walk in obscurity.
Instead my unbridle curiosity will
guide me to my destiny
As I navigate the uncertainty of
this twenty-first century.
---Latoya Hewitt Panton

CHAPTER 4

ENDURING THE JOURNEY

F ast forward twenty years, and here I am crossing over
into a new phase of my life. A phase of hope, prosperity,
and opportunity. For years I had dreamed about traveling,
not just for fun, but also to actually experience the culture
of the people. In my mind culture was everything; separate
from God it was the one thing that could distinguish you,
define you, ignite you, and connect you with others of your
kind or similar spirits. How else could I explain to someone the rhythm in my steps, the natural twist in my hair,
the freedom of my laughter, the confidence of my posture,
the determination in my eyes, the creativity of my cuisine,
and the audacity of my hope if not through culture. It was
the very essence of my natural being. Hence I was ready to
explore this new canvas: a country with a rich history, the

melting pot of diversity, and the embodiment of courage. Furthermore, I was feeling confident after having overcome the worst—the hate, the lies, and the put-downs; all that was behind me now. If anything I would adapt the lessons learned from my past to forge ahead into the future.

THE HOPE OF AMERICA

I eased myself back in the seat of the airplane and got ready for takeoff. I relished the thought of this mechanical bird taking me over massive volumes of water to a land that, though distant in its demographics, was similar in its fight for equality, and justice, and dream for a better tomorrow. In my mind the United States was a great country, from drafting and deploying a million-man army to assisting their Allied forces in World War I, to providing military supplies to Allied forces yet again in World War II, and providing assistance to refugees and immigrants around the world through numerous World Relief organizations. Not to mention, the numerous Christian missionaries who brought modern medicine and set up educational institutions all over the Middle East and around the world. These were just a few testimonials of the true patriotism of this country. I was to now understand what the line, "The land of the free and the home of the brave," in the anthem sang by thousands of Americans on the world stage really meant. For many people America represented hope and prosperity. I have often heard of stories of refugees from the continent of Africa and other parts of the world who had been forced out of their communities or country and made to cross distant lands due to violence. For many, America was their hope.

UNCERTAINTY, SURPRISE! FULFILLMENT!

For a moment, time seemed to stop and allowed me to think about what this journey really meant for me. The hope of offering my family a better life stood fearlessly before my eyes with every passing moment. At times I would momentarily curfew the airplane for anything that seemed suspicious; though happy, I was by no means naive of the times I was living in. It was the era when people took pleasure in blowing themselves and others up for some precious gift of the afterlife. "But not today! No sir!" I reasoned within myself. Not while Aunt Cur's granddaughter was on this airplane. In fact I had prayed so hard for this moment that anyone daring to try to do anything stupid would have suddenly found themselves in a world web of unconsciousness. As I sat motionless in the airplane, I could not help but admire God's beautiful creation. It seemed like the ocean danced to the beat of the radiant skies as it modeled its beauty with the fluffy white clouds for all to see. I was soon pulled back to reality when the air hostess signaled for us to get ready for landing. Landing at the Atlanta airport would bring back memories of my first time in the United States. As expected the airport was super busy with everyone bustling about, trying to navigate their own way. As for me I met up with a cohort of teachers that were on a similar mission. With looks of uncertainty, surprise, and fulfillment, we greeted each other and exchanged pleasantries. My desire to forget the past and look toward the future became more forceful. I realized in that moment that if I had any hope of receiving what God had for me, I was going to have to change my mindset from being fixed to growth. As the weeks rolled on, I was integrated into a new framework of teaching and learning. Though similar to what I had practiced eleven years prior, my clients were different. Their mindsets, culture, awareness, and struggles were different. Having been thoroughly guided by the pros and cons, I felt prepared to undertake my new task. Well, so I thought!

CREATED FOR PURPOSE

In the same way that energy cannot be created or destroyed but can change from one form to another (Sir Isaac Newton, the first law of motion), "God's Purpose cannot be created or destroyed." This I found to be consistent with my journey with God. After my first few weeks teaching in the United States, I was convinced that this was not the place I wanted to be. Everything was so foreign, the people, the cultures, the language. "I must have been delusional," I thought. "What was I thinking? Leaving my family, my friends, and my routes to embark upon this perilous journey," I reasoned within myself. Having survived the first semester on my teaching contract, I realized that there was a higher purpose driving me and wanting me to be there. I remembered speaking to my grandmother and relating to her that I wanted to come back home, hoping that after I explained to her the discomfort I felt that she would offer me some words of comfort, and agree with the idea of me returning home. On the contrary, she was bold to strengthen the point that God must get glory in everything that I do. Hence, I knew at that point that it was senseless arguing with her. In fact she would continue to tell me a million reasons why God had provided this new opportunity for me and that it would be better for me to stay in my position. Little did I know that Aunt Cur was seeing way ahead of me; she had tapped into what God was doing in my life, and so was divinely positioned to instruct me according to God's plan for my life. Hence, I began to deepen my resolve to try to understand what God wanted me to learn, and to accomplish on this journey.

THRIVING IN GOD

Isn't it amazing how spiritually naïve we can be to what God is doing in our lives? As I pressed through each day in my new environment, I felt the uneasiness of being in a foreign land and felt more and more like I had made the wrong decision. Despite the somewhat emotional and financial assistance offered to me by the system, I still felt the sense of disconnectedness. The subtle stares and whispers confirmed what I was feeling inside; only they were not true to what God was really doing in my life. Later on I understand that the stares, and whispers were only distracters that the enemy had set up for me to fall victim to his lies and deceptions. As the weeks rolled on I realized that God was simply building my faith, soon my mindset steadily began to change to make way for this organic experience. It is amazing how God can bring you out of a dark place that you are in, to bring you into a place where you can thrive, and prosper in him. Realizing that God was doing "a new thing," I strengthened my resolve and forged ahead. However, within this new environment, I was foreign to everyone and everything, and I felt completely out of my element, but this was exactly how God had design it. It is in our unfamiliar situations that God becomes most clear to us. It is in our weakness that he is made strong (2 Corinthians 12:10).

THE SHIFTING

As days turn into weeks, and weeks turn into months, I was able to see that there were areas where we shared common interests, such as the love for family, the love for humanity, and the fear of what we did not know. As I sat in the workshops, I could hear warm sentiments, and burst of laughter from the side-bar conversation that seemed to blossom around the room. They jumped at every opportunity to catch up with friends and acquaintances about their love-ones, new ventures, and whatever was going on in their daily lives. They spoke freely about their dissatisfaction within the system; both governmental, and institutional. At that moment I realized that people were people no matter where they came from.

Despite me being able to make connections with my new colleagues, I still felt a sense of disconnectedness. I was still fighting with my own thoughts of, "Why would God have pulled me from the known to the unknown?"

As I continued to try to unravel the mystery of God's plans, church became my sustainable force. I would hear the confirming voice of God through the preacher as he encouraged us to be patient as God had something in store for those who waited on him. The thought of how God could strategically shift your circumstances to come into alignment with what he wanted was simply, mind-blowing. I had to accept my new environment and get ready for the continued move of God as he redesigned my mindset.

WALKING ON WATER

Let me first say that prior to this massive change in my environment I thought of myself as a very adventurous person. Someone, who was not oppose to changes, a matter of fact I embrace it. But the level of change that I was experiencing at this moment in my life was like being on a roller coaster ride, being tossed like a pancake, and being ran over by a lawn mower. This spiritual experience would serve to reshape and redesign my whole view of who God is. This new environment reminded me of the story of Peter in the New Testament. At first, when Peter stepped out of the boat and began to walk on water toward Jesus, he had absolute confidence in God. However, when he saw the wind, he became afraid and doubtful and began to sink. According to Mathew 14:29–30, "Come," he said.

Then Peter got down out of the boat, walked on the water, and came toward Jesus. But when he saw the wind boisterous, he was afraid; and beginning to sink, he cried, saying, Lord, save me.

Here we see that when Peter began to make sense of the situation, fear kicked in and crippled him. As a result, he began to sink. The question here is: What caused Peter's faith to shift? Based on the text, Peter sank when he took his eyes off Jesus. Here I was having to learn that same lesson of understanding what it really meant to trust God. How easy is it to say we "trust" God when our circumstances are somewhat normal, or when we are in our familiar environment? This new experience taught me that our true trust in God can only be fully explored when we are place in unfamiliar waters.

REFLECTION

From time to time God tends to put us in situations where we feel like we are literally, "Walking on Water." Have you had the "Peter Experience?" What were your thoughts as you stepped into the unknown?

THE CULTURE SHOCK

I remember my first day on the job like it was yesterday. Students teased at my every word, underestimated my authority, and questioned my nationality. I remember one student asking me, "So do you have pizza in Jamaica," while another echoed, "How did you get here? Do you have cars in Jamaica?" As I looked at their innocent faces anticipating my next word, I felt a sense of duty to educate and bring awareness about my country—Jamaica. It was at that point I knew my job had been fixed. Like Mars and Jupiter, my students' awareness of where I had come from was far-fetched and vague. They did not think I knew what a pizza looked like, let alone would be able to identify a fast-food restaurant like McDonald's and Wendy's or even Subway. Their ideas of the island of paradise were broken-down buildings, zinc fences, donkeys, and camels. How was I going to bring awareness to my students? How was I going to effectively paint the picture of the country revered by so many? This was to be the beginning of a new cultural revolution for both myself and my students.

Jamaica is known by many as the land of "wood and water." It's said to have been discovered by Christopher Columbus on May 3, 1494. The country was first taken over by the Spaniards. However, British fought the Spaniards and the country was won over by the British in 1645. Jamaica gained independence from Great Britain on August 6, 1962.

The term "culturally responsive pedagogy" is a term used in education to describe a strategy that encourages educators to use the cultural experiences of their students to assist students in core content areas. Culture affects all aspects of a school. It influences informal conversations in the faculty lunchroom, the type of instruction valued, and how professional knowledge is viewed (Deal and Peterson, 2016, p. 14). This supported the need for me to learn more about my students' culture in order to connect with them socially, emotionally, and educationally.

During the coming months, we would begin our cultural exchange, which consisted first of our conception of what we knew about each other. This would lead to them telling me about their favorite game, "basketball," and their favorite basketball players. I soon realized that one of their main staples was mac and cheese and fried chicken. In return, I shared with them some of my most loved Jamaican dishes. Epitomized by the pictures of Jamaican cuisine such as curried chicken and white rice, oxtails and rice and peas, and ackee and saltfish with fried dumplings, I would soon transition from being called the "foreign teacher" to the "Jamaican teacher." I capitalized on the opportunity to share more of my culture with them. They beamed with excitement as I shared videos of our dance, music, and sports. I remember showing the students a video of Usain Bolt winning the one hundred meters in Beijing, China, in the 2012 Olympics. Not only did he win the race but he also had set a new world record of 9.69 seconds. Like the bright lights in the national stadiums, their faces lit up with curiosity and excitement! They wanted to know more about him, they wanted to know more about the sports we played in Jamaica, and they wanted to experience more of our culture. At this point I recognized that we had found a common ground—the things we cherished. Thereafter, I transitioned from being an international teacher working in the United States to become an ambassador for Jamaica, the land of wood and water. As the opportunities would present themselves for me to share my culture with my students and the wider school community, it gave me a deeper sense of purpose and self. Helping people to understand my culture ignited in me a new passion which would continue to grow in the coming months.

REFLECTION

For centuries culture has played a vital role in the social-ization of the human species. What aspects of your cul-ture do you believe have been most impactful on others?

FEAR OF THE UNKNOWN

In the words of Andrew Smith, "People fear what they don't understand and hate what they can't conquer."

This I found to be true among the students I served and a lot of other persons whom I came in contact with. It was not that they did not want to learn about other peo-ple and cultures, but they were fearful of what they did not know or understand. As a result, they did not know how to receive this new awakening, this new paradigm shift. For my students it was like a new wave of consciousness had intercepted their Orion, and I was blessed with the opportunity to become their astrologer as we navigated the universe of culture and diversity within our own sphere. I guess this was God's way of letting me know that he had a higher purpose for me. I began to buy into the idea of this new revolution and see myself as a prospective catalyst of change.

MAKING CONNECTIONS

If at first you don't succeed, try and try and try again
--Frederick Marryat

There were many things that I did not succeed in, and there were some things that I thought I could have been better at. However, having the ability to see the good in people despite the negative circumstances would make all the difference in the world. Someone once told me, "You do not need to be good at everything; you only needed to be good at one thing." At first when I heard it, I began to ponder, "Why should I only try to be good at one thing when I could learn so many things." As I continue to search for the meaning in this new epiphany, I realized that if you could be good at one thing then you would not need to worry about all the other things that you weren't so good at. While adapting to my unfamiliar place, I found that one thing that I was good at -- humor. I noticed that my students would always want me to speak in my Jamaican dialect, not to actually learn the language but for the humor they found in it. I found that if I could make my students laugh, that I could win their hearts forever. We made fun out of the simplest things. Sometimes during the lesson, one of the students would inject his own definition of what he thought I said, and the whole class would just go berserk. I remembered trying to squash an argument that seemed to have reached over one hundred degrees Fahrenheit though the thermostat was showing seventy-five degrees Fahrenheit. One student, who I will refer to as Billy, had called another student, Harry, out of his name, which was a regular energy booster for them. The thought of being called "an overgrown cockroach" did not resonate that well with Harry. So I interjected by saying, "Everyone has something about themselves they are not comfortable with!"

In no time, another student yelled from the back of the room; "Yeah like your unibrow." Instantly I clapped back, "You didn't hear me calling you the hairy monster!"

The entire class catapulted into laughter. That day commenced the start of new beginnings. Students realized that offense is never given, only taken.

My students and I cultivated an atmosphere where everyone felt a sense of belonging. It did not matter their abilities or lack thereof. What was important was to make sure everybody felt appreciated and loved.

CULTURAL DISCRIMINATION

People will forget what you said, people
will forget what you did, but people will
never forget how you made them feel
—Maya Angelou

This quote held a lot of truth for me as I began to reflect on the moments when I felt like quitting. My feeling of quitting did not come from a belief that I did not have the ability to do the job. Neither did it come from a lack of understanding of who I was, but it came from the feeling I felt when I knew I was treated wrongly, disrespected, and alienated. Having a philosophical nature, I would always try to understand why people would try to be so mean and heartless. Like what made them do it—what was that driving force? I soon realized that it wasn't me. But instead it had to do with their own biases and prejudices that were hidden deep inside their souls. I remember having to take my sick five-year-old to school wrapped in a towel because he had a cold and fever. When I called in and asked if I could get some time off to take my child to the doctor, the response was, "We don't have coverage for your class." I found out later that another colleague had made that same request and was allowed to be out for a week with her sick child. From that day I had lost all respect for that kind of leadership. I quickly allowed forgiveness to reign in my heart to avoid the ugly stain of hate and resentment that emanate from the system. Later, I would find out that I wasn't the only one who had experienced this level discrimination and bias. That year would stand out in my memory as one of the most life-changing moments in my life. Not because of any hallmark moment of human kindness bestowed to me by others, but because of the subtle thread of discrimination and bias that I and many others experienced.

REFLECTION

Racial, social, and cultural discrimination exist in all sectors of our society. How has any of these forms of discrimination affected you?

CULTURAL STEREOTYPES

Please allow me to address quite briefly the impact of culture on a persons' social construct. It would be somewhat impossible for me to pen this book without looking sharply at the role that cultural sensitivity or the lack there of played in my experience as an international educator. The concept of cultural identify is defined as a person's individual image of the cultural features that characterize his or her group and the reflection of these features in his or her self-representation (Madsen & Mabokata,2005). Being foreign allowed me to see how xenophobic people were and how this world was. This familiar monster would demonstrate itself in the occasional cattiness and total disregard for the people who serve on the frontline from other countries. What was interesting was that this cultural bias did not just exist among small pockets of individual, but it was displayed in the very leadership style at the top of the administration. At that point I defined for myself what leadership meant by identifying all the things that true leadership was not. Leadership was not about discriminating against other minority groups, leadership was not about demeaning others, and leadership was certainly not about dictating or controlling your followers. Instead leadership at its core was about love, kindness, hope, equity, and connectedness. Leading with heart means understanding love in the context of leadership and putting relationship and connectedness at the center of our leadership practice (East,2018). In reality this kind of leadership did not just have an adverse effect on educators from foreign countries, but on children from other ethnic groups as well. Being in this environment I noticed that students from minority groups often complained of being bullied by other students, as well as being treated differently because of their cultural background. Lack of sensitivity to these factors can adversely affect students' participation and academic performance. Hence, it is important for us to check our own bias and prejudices of others before we take on leadership positions. In the words of Mohandas Gandhi, "Be the change that you want to see in the world."

REFLECTION

Transformational leadership is a familiar phrase in education. What are some attributes of a true leader?

ACTIVITY
STOP-AND-THINK

1. What are two positive effects of culture?
2. Write two attributes of a good leader?
3. Explain why good leadership is important

DOUBT

Doubt—she goes around stifling weak souls,
meek souls, hurt souls, great souls.

Doubt—she is void of understanding,
defies all logic and knowledge.
With her dead beats, she marches on like
a prey in the path of her predator.
Hoping to find solace in her loss of existence and
power.
Doubt—never doubt her ability to devour.
Meek souls, weak souls, great souls, she will conquer.
---Latoya Hewitt Panton

CHAPTER 5

DRASTIC TIMES CALLS FOR DRASTIC MEASURES

M ake sure to wash your hands, stock up on Lysol, and avoid touching your face with your hands.

These were just a few tips buzzing in the atmosphere as the world battled the pandemic of the coronavirus. This was an unpresented time in our world, and people from all countries had one common thread—surviving the COVID-19 pandemic.

Years prior during my time of deep reflection, I realized that if I were to maintain my existence in this life, I would need to take some drastic measures that would help to save the existence of not only my life but also the lives of my close friends and family. Like to survive the coronavirus pandemic,

I needed to sanitize myself daily. I also realized that I needed to sanitize myself spiritually to get rid of spiritual viruses that would try to attach themselves to me. Whereas the coronavirus is said to have originated from animals and then later transmitted to human beings, hate, jealousy, and resentment stem from the devil. We are reminded in the Bible that hate, resentment, strife, malice, and the like are all sinful works of the flesh. However, the coronavirus and sinful fleshly tendencies have one major thing in common—their infectious quality. The infectious nature of the coronavirus is similar to how the negative attitudes of humans spread from one to another. Like the coronavirus, when a negative energy, or spirit, emerges, we as humans tend to lack the immunity to fight it off. Hence, if not treated carefully, we become infected, and the negative spirits spread to others around us. One of the attributes of a virus is that it must use host cells to create more virions. However, many claim that the coronavirus cannot survive in warm temperatures, so when exposed to warm air, it tends to die. In retrospect, I understand that I needed to activate more effectively the spiritual antidote given to me by God through his word to fight the spiritual diseases such as unforgiveness, hate, resentment, the pride of life, and the evil ambitions. I have had experiences where people have demonstrated so much hate and resentment that it made them stagnant in their lives, and in the end they suffered from setbacks, failures in relationships, and depression. They were always so focused on ruining the other person that they themselves never aspired to greatness.

REFECTION

It is said that over 219 virus species have been known to affect humans in some way or another. What sort of spiritual antidote are you using to fight off spiritual viruses?

THE CINDERELLA EXPERIENCE

In the story of Cinderella and her stepsister and stepmother, Cinderella was put at a disadvantage because her mother died and soon her father died, leaving her with her cruel stepmother and coldhearted sisters. Their hate was fueled by jealousy for Cinderella. Imagine being treated like you are a nobody everyday of your life! Always being picked at by others; who resented you and treated you like trash. And if that was not enough, they would tell lies on you all the time. Instead of being vindicated, you were slapped with extra chores. And when Cinderella wanted to attend the ball, her stepmother says she can go, "if" she can complete all her chores, and "if" she can find something suitable to wear. One would wonder if there was any hope for Cinderella. But as the story unfolds, we saw where Cinderella's fairy godmother saved the day using a few of her tricks. Later on we saw that Cinderella showed up at the ball with the help of her fairy godmother and met the prince, who fell in love with her. The prince later married Cinderella, and they lived happily ever after, whereas the jealous stepsisters were left totally humiliated and miserable. The morale of the story in the end is "good always overcomes evil." The story of Cinderella is the reality for many of us today. But it is comforting to know that out of the darkest of situations in our life, if we maintain a positive attitude, God will also work things out for our good. Romans 8:28 states, "And we know that in all things God works for the good of those who love him, who have been called according to his purpose." Though we may not have a fairy godmother like Cinderella, we have a heavenly Father who is all knowing, and whose eyes go to and fro, observing the ways of men. Hence, for us to get the best of what our heavenly Father has for us, it is important that we rid ourselves of the negative energy that causes pain, resentment and unforgiveness.

ATTITUDE VERSES ALTITUDE

Charting the course to success depends heavily on your attitude. I have often heard the saying, "Your attitude determines your altitude." I find this statement to be exceptionally true. The story is told of the "The Rhinoceros and the Bird," the rhinoceros was always grumpy and had a negative attitude toward life. This was mostly because he was always plagued by bugs and ants who were always on his back. The rhinoceros was similar to that "bully" at school whom everybody was afraid of and did not want to be around. The little bird somehow saw his plight and decided to assist him. Now, the rhino could have taken the approach of "don't tell me what to do" or "you act like you can solve everybody's problem!" and dismissed the bird. But instead he decided to listen to what the bird had to say. So the bird later made a proposal where he would get rid of the bugs off the rhino's back by eating them, and then in turn he could ride on the rhino's back for free. Talk about driving a good bargain. Well if the rhino agreed he would not be so grumpy anymore, and all the other animals would not be hating on him. You see the rhinoceros's attitude toward the bird would make all the difference in the world. As expected the rhino accepted the offer and found that he was a whole lot happier for it. His ability to listen to others helped to improve his quality or life and also helped him to have a more peaceful life. You see people will always try to capitalize on our weakness. However, our ability to accept our weaknesses and tackle them head on will save us unnecessary stress. I can just imagine how shocked the other animals must have been to see the rhino happy; because in their eyes there was no way that he could have gotten any relief from those bugs. Another epiphany I got from this story is that help sometimes comes from the most unexpected places. How could the rhino ever have guessed that a little bird could solve his problems. This supports the view that God can use the most simple or miniature things in our life to turn our circumstances around.

REFLECTION

"But God chose the foolish things of the world to shame the wise; God chose the weak things of the world to shame the strong," (1Corinthians 2:27).

God tends to use the simplest things in our lives to teach us valuable lessons. What is one thing that God has used in your life that totally blew your mind?

FIXED MINDSET VERSES GROWTH MINDSET

We can change our attitude by changing our mindset from fixed to growth. Allow me to pause for a moment as I unpack the true meaning of the terms Fixed and Growth Mindset. I believe the first time I heard the terms fixed and growth mindset was five years ago. I was at a professional development workshop geared towards assisting educators to assist student with special needs in the general education classroom. The presenter was a very flamboyant male teacher who I will refer to as Carl, who had been teaching students with special needs for a number of years. His keynote was on the topic, "How to have a Growth Mindset." At first I wondered how in the world having a growth mindset was connected to teaching students with reading disability in the inclusive environment. However, as he began to share nuggets of his experience with us we were able to see the connection. You see, Carl was the father of a fifteen year old child who I will refer to as Johnny; who had been struggling academically for years. Though he knew his child was smart he was still seeing inconsistencies in his academic results. Carl shared with us that as Johnny moved from one class to the next that he kept getting the same results-- below average. Seeing these results prompted him and his wife to seek help for his son; which meant getting Johnny tested. The test results confirmed that Johnny had Dyslexia. Dyslexia is a term used to describe a disorder that makes it difficult for a child to read and interpret words. However, instead of giving up Carl decided to adapt a "growth mindset" approach. This approach would help him and his wife create the right learning environment for Jonny. As Carl began to provide the support that Johnny needed, he and his wife began to see positive gains. Johnny began to do much better on his test, and had a positive attitude towards his education. Carl attributed this success with Johnny to having a growth mindset. It is so easy for us to sometimes throw in the towel when we come up on a hurdle. But sometimes all the situation requires is having a positive or growth mindset. Standing in Carl's shoe allowed me to realize that the situation with Johnny was not easy to deal with. He and his wife could have easily accepted their fate and moved along, but instead they sought solutions to the problem. They did not adapt a fixed mindset, but instead they chose to have a growth mindset which gave them a better outcome. Daily affirmations such as "I can do all things through Christ who strengthens me," "I can't" to "I will try." and "I was made to conquer, not to wobble in defeat," are all positive mindset tools that we can adapt to deal with the challenges we face in our lives.

REFLECTION

It is said that challenges come to make us stronger. How do you tackle challenges or hurdles in your daily life?

USING THE TOOLS OF EDUCATION

Having a positive mindset, allows us to use the tool of education to create pathways of upliftment and enlightenment that can further help to develop our future goals. In the words of Nelson Mandela, "Education is the key that can unlock any door." Education provides the vehicle we need for success and to make a life-changing impact on others. With this in mind, I realized that I could fight ignorance with education, fear with perseverance, curiosity with exploration, and poverty with determination. Fulfilling purpose and destiny required taking serious measures. It required the tenacity of a lion and the ferociousness of a bulldog to overcome and fight the spiritual and physical challenges of life. With every new opportunity that presented itself for me to improve my knowledge and gain new skills and insight, there was never a moment "as the right timing." Instead I had to seize the moment. The time to take on new ventures always seemed off. I was always met with financial challenges, uncertainties, and spiritual battles. One would think that having the right setting and support mechanism is the key to becoming successful and achieving one's goal, but I have found that success for many is not dependent on a perfect or conducive environment. Instead, it depends on one's will power, hard work, and positive connectivity to overcome life challenges. Furthermore, it requires a certain kind of spiritual muscle that can only be achieved through the challenges and experiences we go through. The spiritual battles seemed to provide the fuel I needed to press forward. And with every negative situation that presents itself, I believed that there is a positive seed that will spring forth.

REFLECTION

Education is the key to unlock the golden door of freedom (George Washington Carver)

In what ways have education helped you to accomplish your dreams?

ADAPTING TO MY ENVIRONMENT

I soon realized that my journey to success not only depended on my attitude, but it also depended on my ability to adapt to my environment. This I could do in a way that would not just help to plummet my success but would also serve to defy the fear of thinking I was not strong enough. In my quest to understand the secret to adaptation, I pounced upon the willow ptarmigan. These birds, Alaska's state pride, are some of the most interesting and beautiful birds you could ever find. In the winter their all-white covering camouflages them and protects them from predators. During this time they nibble on willow trees for food. Furthermore, it is even difficult to tell male and female apart. However, during the spring and summer months, these babies know how to stir it up. They molt and shed their furs. Aside from mating and laying five to fourteen eggs a day, they are also privy to a variety to fruits, twigs, and flowers, which constitute their daily diet. What I found most interesting about these birds was their new feathers that were brown with gold and black mixed in.

My ability to camouflage myself with my surroundings would make all the difference in my life and future endeavors. This ability helped to preserve me in my unfamiliar surroundings. How did I accomplish this? While I hasten to tell you that there was no magic formula, neither was there any magic wand that helped me to see beyond my current situation. It took deep reflection and constantly reminding myself of the goal ahead. During this time I looked for the good in every circumstance. When greeted with sour grapes, I turned them into wine; when swarmed by the bees, I excreted the honey; and when I came up on a red light, I waited patiently for the green light to come on. Like the ptarmigans I had to wait for the right season to shed my fur so I could gather new and fresh feathers. In my own case, that meant the birthing of new ideas, new purpose, and new vision.

REFLECTION

As you look back in your life was there ever a time when you had to adapt to your environment to fit in? Did this adaption change who you are?

HARNESSING THE MOMENT

The story is told of a boy in Malawi whose ability to "harness the wind" helped to provide food for his family and community. His perseverance against the naysayers would not just afford him the opportunity to build more windmills but would also provide him the opportunity to later come to the United States to visit other wind farms and to go to college. In my own sphere I had to find a way to seize the moment when faced with difficult circumstances. Putting it plainly, "I had to Capture The Moment." Though at times I was not in an ideal setting, I found a way to use the opportunity to work toward my goals and aspirations. That meant sacrificing, time management, and determination. I remember tooth-pulling days of trying to juggle the task of writing this book, along with a million and one other tasks. Thoughts of quitting were the easiest option on the menu board. However, my supportive spouse and remembering the reason why I started in the first place kept me wanting to complete the mission. Some days I only had the luxury of three to four hours of sleep, but this was just what I needed to carry out my duties throughout the day. During this time I realize that God will sometimes give us just what we need to survive. Similar to the people of Israel who traveled forty years in the wilderness, God supplied them with a measured amount of manna for each day. In addition, he had given specific instruction to the Israelites to eat only the manna they had gathered for each day. However, as is the nature of human beings, we tend to store up more than we need and not listen to instruction when first given. The Israelites would soon realize the effects of their actions, as the food soon became spoiled and they had to throw it away. Hence my specific task in that season was to harness the moment, which meant seeing the opportunity at the right time and seizing it once again. Furthermore, my mindset of what I thought I needed would become irrelevant during this time; instead it was my ability to fulfill purpose and destiny that would become my driving force.

STAYING STRONG

Heights by great men reached and kept
were not attained by sudden flight but
they while their companions slept were
toiling upward through the night.
---Henry Wadsworth

This was just one of the poems that my classmates and I would have to recite every day. Sometimes it would be in the morning before we started class, sometimes it was after our first morning break, and sometimes it was just before going home. Ms. Campbell would ensure that we recited this quote religiously while attending her class. The more we said it was the more we believed it. And the more we believed it, the more we began to demonstrate it in our work, in our attitude, and in our desire for excellence. In my present state, I would begin to see the connection of my past experience as a student to my current situation. I would have to apply the same principles to overcome the giants that stood in my way. I would have to persevere; I would have to overcome the challenges ahead if I were to become successful and defeat the Goliaths in my life. Facing my diverse trials and tribulation was not what would determine my destiny, but it was what would lead me to it. However, my attitude while going through the fire, while going through the flood, and while going through the earthquake would determine my altitude once again. Oftentimes in the Bible, the Lord reminded the people of Israel, "When you pass through the waters I will be with you; and through the rivers, they shall not overflow you. When you walk through the fire you shall not be burned nor shall the flames scotch you." I must confess that I did not understand what this meant until I had to endure tribulation and walk through hate, negativity, and setbacks. God would expect me to remain strong and hold on to his words. However, it was easier to read the scriptures than to apply them to my life when I passed through the trying times. I would come to learn that this was God's expectation for my life. Furthermore, staying strong in diverse tribulation meant that I had to pass through pain and suffering.

Pain and suffering stood out as two of the spiritual sharpeners of the Christian faith. The Word of God reminds us that, "he was wounded for our transgressions, he was bruised for our iniquities: the chastisement of our peace was upon him; and with his stripes we are healed" (Isaiah 53:5). Hence, the need to remain strong was mandatory.

ACTIVITY
STOP-AND-THINK-

> But he was wounded for our transgressions, he was bruised for our iniquities: the chastisement of our peace was upon him; and with his stripes we are healed (Isaiah 53: 5)

The scripture above is a familiar verse to Christians around the world.

1. How do the words of this scripture connect to your Christian journey with Christ?
2. Why did Christ have to go through all this for us?

The Uncreated Creator

He is uncontrollable, irresistible,
untamable, and undeniable.
Who is he who controls the reservoirs of the sea?
Who is he who sits upon the circle of the earth?
He is the uncreated creator, the
unmoved mover of all creation.
---Latoya Panton

CHAPTER 6

UNDERSTANDING THE MIND OF GOD

Over the years God would show me that he is unlimited. He is unlimited in his perspective, in his vision, in his plans, in his ways. I recall years ago when I came to the United States. God reminded me in his words that, "His ways are higher than my ways and his thoughts are higher than my thoughts; As the heavens are higher than the earth so are his thoughts higher than my thoughts and his ways higher than my ways" (Isaiah 43:2). But understanding the "how" would make all the difference in the world for me. Looking back, I saw many times when God would just blow my mind and remind me that he is God. I remembered having completed college and wanting to pursue my first degree. I decided to return to the same college I attended previously (St. Joseph's

Teachers' College), a familiar place I knew. It made perfect sense to me at the time. Why would I need to go to another college or institution that I was not familiar with? I assured myself that this must have been God's plan for me. Well that was what I thought. I made my first down payment and was to commence my degree program in the fall. While attending the college, I would realize that even though it was the same institution that I attended years ago, something was just off. First, I would struggle to leave work to get to class on time. When I got to the class I struggled to connect. It was like I was locked into a dark room with no way of escaping. Day after day I would make the sacrifice and show up on time. However, it became more and more daunting because I just was not able to juggle the time effectively. I soon realized that was not the path that God was leading me on. Consequently, I had to make the tough choice, which meant making a U-turn. It's funny how sometimes you think you are making a foolish decision to quit something you started only to find out that it was the best decision you ever made. In my head I was going to lose my money, my time, and my sacrifice, not realizing that delay did not mean denial. Little did I know that God had a bigger plan. Later on I was to find out through my colleague about another university that was offering the same program with more flexible hours. This opportunity afforded me the possibility of managing and scheduling my time in a way that suited my situation. It was like a breath of fresh air.

Understanding the
Spiritual Perspective

It's interesting how God can redirect your entire life to realize his purpose and his plan for your life. I was so busy focusing on the physical challenges that I lost sight of the spiritual perspective. Hence, in my mind this was not going to be possible. As the weeks rolled on, I became more and more convinced that this was the path I should take. I summoned up the courage and enrolled within that same year. God would blow my mind over and over as he would provide the tuition on time every time. Every time there was a need, he would supply. I realized through that experience that God was indeed a waymaker. He was not like the weather—he did not change. He was not like the dollar: he could not devalue. And he was not like a man: he could not lie, neither was he propelled by his emotions. He did not change. God wants his people to see as he sees. He is able to fight our battles if we trust his words. He reminded me in Isaiah 42:8, "I am the Lord, that is my name; And My glory I will not give to another." This was consistent with the fact that God was going to get the glory out of my life no matter what. It didn't matter whether I believed in myself, or whether others believed in me. What was important was what God said about me.

> ### REFLECTION
>
> It's amazing how we tend to put limitations on our-
> selves. We tend to carve out in stone the things that
> we can and cannot do. How have you limited your-
> self in the past? What did you discover about your-
> self now that you did not recognize then?

BE STRONG AND COURAGEOUS

"I can do all things through Christ who strengthens me"
(Philippians 4:13) is one of the most quoted scriptures in the
Christian community. It is the undercurrent that drives the
ambitions and aspirations of many successful people in our
world today. However, it has proven to be easier said than
done. A story is told in the book of Exodus about Moses's
encounter with God. The people of Israel had been suffering many years under the harsh dictates of the Egyptians, and
their cry had come up to God. Moses was the chosen servant
who would be sent to deliver the children of Israel from their
oppressors. During the course of time, God would have many
encounters with Moses. But Moses's first encounter with God
is what stood out so strongly for me. God had given Moses
specific instructions to carry out when he met with the people
of Israel and with the Pharaoh. In God's eyes Moses had all
the prerequisites of a strong leader: he was a Hebrew, he was
passionate about his people, and he had the tenacity of a lion.

However, upon meeting with the almighty God, the uncreated creator, the "I Am that I Am," Moses did not believe in his ability to speak what the Lord had told him.

MOSES THE STUTTERER

Exodus 4:10 states, "Then Moses said to the Lord, O my Lord, I am not eloquent, neither before nor since You have spoken to Your servant; but I am slow of speech and slow of tongue." This has been my typical response to God many times when he would instruct me to minister to someone, or move in a particular direction. Like Moses I just could not understand why of all the people in the world he could choose to do his work, he would choose me. I would tend to find every reason why I was not suitable for the task. I often tend to look at what people were going to say about me. I feared being criticized, I feared being isolated, and I feared being stigmatized. It would not be long before I realized that God did not care about that and that I was only limiting myself in God.

DO NOT GRIEVE THE HOLY SPIRIT

Countless times I would have to ask God to forgive me for not doing what he instructed me to do. I remembered telling God on one occasion that he is making me feel like an "old woman." While my peers were enjoying themselves, partying and having fun, I was busy preaching and sharing God's

Word in the buses, on the streets, and to anyone who would listen. My constant complaining would drive away the Spirit of God and left me feeling empty. It was like someone had taken out all of my insides and left only my skeleton. I felt empty; I felt lost. In my desperation I cried out to God to refill me with his Spirit and to move upon me once again. It would take daily crying, fasting, and seeking God for me to feel his presence once more. From that moment I was sure that as the sun lights the day and the moon lights the night, I was not going to act in rebellion against the Holy Spirit again. In that moment I realized that God was real and that his glory he will not share with another.

REFLECTION

Like Moses we tend to find excuses to avoid doing what God has commanded us to do. In what ways are you like Moses?

ALL THINGS WORK TOGETHER FOR GOOD

How would you describe an entrepreneur, a multibillionaire, or even a soccer player? Successful? Smart? Genius? You likely would not say the same about someone who is faced with harsh circumstances, doesn't know where his or her next meal is coming from, and is facing the sad reality of being evicted. The truth is, while these two kinds of people may be different for obvious reasons, they share a common thread that is undeniable. They both possess the potential to acquire wealth. As I forged ahead, one thing that became clear to me was that we were all created for a purpose, and finding that purpose and being able to fulfill that purpose makes all the difference in our lives. The good book says, "All things work together for good to them that love God and are called according his purpose" (Romans 8:28). This shows that whatever situations we find ourselves in, God will eventually work it out for our good. Without our experiences we would not have a testimony. Without our experiences we would not be able to identify with others. Without our experiences we would not have compassion for others. I remember years ago my mother encouraged me to go on missions with members of my church to the prison. Here I was thinking that she must have been completely insane to suggest that idea. In my own mind prison was a place filled with murderers, rapists, thieves, pedophiles, and such the like. Why should I go to visit them? After much persuasion I finally agreed to go. Upon arriving at the prison and seeing all these young, middle aged, and old men just wasting away, I instantly felt a sense of compassion. It seemed as if God just transformed my stony heart in flesh. I was able to see how he sees. I was able to look beyond the fault and see the need. As I along with other church members began to minister to these men, I recognize that some of them really wanted salvation. On the other hand, some looked with skepticism, and resentment to the gospel. As weeks rolled on we would hear of the many experiences that brought them to prison. They were on different journeys- some were serving ten year sentences, some fifteen to twenty year sentences, while others were serving life sentences. As I thought about their different experiences, I realized that God was in control of their lives. Their scheduled had been reshuffled in a way that allowed them to meet and hear from God. One of the prisoners whom we had met on our missions was released and had made a 360 degree turn around in his life. Today I still thank God for this experience because I came to understand that God is a God of judgment, but that he is also a God of compassion.

REFLECTION

But when he saw the multitudes, he was moved with compassion on them, because they fainted, and were scattered abroad, as sheep having no shepherd. Think of a time when you experienced the compassion of Jesus Christ. Maybe you felt you did not deserve it but He showed you compassion anyway. How did that moment make you feel?

BEING AMONG THE REMNANT

A lot can be said about taking on a new challenge or trying something new for the first time. You tend to have mixed emotions and feelings of being timid, anxious, and even uncertain about what to expect. For many people, traveling outside their country for the first time can be a very traumatizing yet life-changing experience. For many it would require them to do a bit of research about the place they are traveling to. Similarly, if you are learning to drive a car, you may need to sign up for driving lessons, purchase a driving book, or even get a car manual to understand how it functions. However, to understand who God is, the most important thing you need is knowing the word of God, and the ability to hear God's voice and respond appropriately.

In the book of Exodus chapter 3, we see where God presented himself in the burning bush to Moses. Upon getting Moses's attention, he began to call out to him, "Moses! Moses!"

Moses's ability to respond to God by following specific instructions was important to him experiencing God on a higher spiritual level.

One might ask the question: Where is my life going? Or what is God's plan for my life? Part of the answer lies in the book of Isaiah chapter 11. Here God talks about the "remnant:" "It shall come to pass in that day That the Lord shall set His hand again the second time To recover the remnant of His people who are left" (Isaiah 11:10–11). In Isaiah we realized that the remnants were precious in God's sight. These were people that, though at times they would fall from grace by not being able to live up to certain principles and precepts of God's Word, they would soon discover their mistakes and return to God. Though many of them were scattered at times to different countries and cities, God never lost track or sight of them. It is very important to know that God will never lose sight or track of us despite our shortcomings. God is omnipresent, meaning he is everywhere at the same time, so he knows just when and where to locate us. Whereas in our present world, if people go missing, they would try to track their steps by finding out who last spoke with them or what they were wearing, or try to get access to their cell phones to track their messages. Moreover, our tech giants of today have made it even easier to locate people by implementing a tracking system in their cell phones. On the contrary our God does not need all those additional tools because he is the ultimate human tracker. Hence, being among the "remnant" of almighty God is to know that God will locate us in our given season and perfect that which concerns us for his glory and honor. It is also knowing that God has a plan for our lives even though at times we do not understand what that looks like or is; God is still in control and will fulfill his purpose in our lives.

REFLECTION

"In that day the Lord of host will be a crown of glory, and a diadem of beauty, to the remnant of his people" Isaiah 28:5

What does it really mean to be among the remnant of God?

GOD, OUR LORD AND MASTER

Who in this world knows our sitting down and our rising up? Who understands our thoughts from far off? Who formed our inward parts and covered us in our mother's womb? Only God.

Who in this world can cover us when we cannot cover ourselves? Only God.

Proverbs 3:19 states, "The Lord by wisdom founded the earth; by understanding he established the heavens." Hence God is able to understand us more than we could ever understand ourselves because he is God.

As we look back in the book of Exodus 24:9–18, we see where God rested on Mount Sinai so much so that the cloud covered the mountain for six days. When I thought about this, I realized that God was very strategic in how he related to the people of Israel. When God visits his people, there is direct evidence of his presence. This means that he gives us enough time to recognize who he is and to get ourselves ready to commune with him. When God reaches down to connect with the sons of men, he is getting ready to do a new thing. Moreover, he is getting ready to make an everlasting transformation.

HE IS THE GOD THAT TEARS, BUT HE ALSO MENDS

Isn't it funny how in the most unfortunate situation, the blessing of God is present? God can use the most embarrassing, failing, and dead situation for a triumphant testimonial that can restore your life or the life of someone else. We often hear the saying "out of evil comes good." When we look in the good book, we see where the people of Israel examine their ways before God, but they also examined God's faithfulness toward them. In the book of Hosea 6:1, the people of Israel said, "Though He has torn us he will heal us." God is an awesome God; though he has torn us, he will also heal us; though he has wounded us, he will also heal us. Though sometimes we question why God would allow certain things to happen to us, how can a good God allow bad things to happen to us, I have come to realize that God's ways are past finding out. We cannot understand the mind of God because he is infallible, infinite. Many times in my life, when God moved in an unfamiliar way, I would question the reason for his move. I would spend countless hours trying to understand the meaning and purpose of his actions. Later, he would bring me back to the realization that his ways are past finding out. Therefore, all he required me to do was to trust him.

DO NOT RETURN FROM FOLLOWING AFTER GOD

Oftentimes we hear people talk about a particular member of their family as being an outcast and unruly or being the "black sheep of the family." Well how does one become the black sheep of the family? It could be that we are not certain about our purpose and spiritual importance in the family. As a result, we tend to deviate from the family values or norms. Some of the negative consequences of being the black sheep of the family are that you may be written off by family members and lose your position and inheritance in the family. You may also be scarred emotionally, socially, and psychologically, and you may also lose your identity and become disconnected from your roots. But where there are negative consequences, there are also some positive consequences. Being the black sheep of the family, you may find that you have a greater sense of awareness and preservation of self. You may be more independent of others and able to perceive the pitfalls in your life as well as in others. You may be even more prone to seek restoration and healing for your emotional and spiritual wounds. In the book of Exodus 32:7–14, we saw where the Lord cast off the people of Israel because the people had created for themselves a molded calf to worship and to sacrifice to. They had turned away from following God's principles and walked after their own fleshly desires. As a result, God's anger burned against them, so much so that he contemplated consuming them. Throughout the scriptures, we can see many more episodes of Israel's defiance toward God's principles and precepts. However, there were always remnants of the Lord who would often recognize their waywardness and seek forgiveness and restoration. Sometimes, as the black sheep of the family, others in the family may even think of destroying us because of our unconscionable actions. But with the people of Israel, God showed compassion on his people and refrained from destroying them. It is my hope that if we find ourselves outside the will of God, we will seek restoration and run back to the all-knowing, all powerful God who can redeem us from our sins.

REFLECTION

Gideon thought of himself as the black sheep of the family. According to him, "my clan is the weakest in Manasseh, and I am the least in my father's house" (Judges 6: 15).

How do you view yourself in your own family? What if God wanted to use you to deliver your family member, relatives or someone you knew out of trouble? What would your initial response be?

LIFE IN THE SPIRIT REALMS

Jesus answered and said to them, "Destroy this temple, and in three days I will raise it up"
—John 2:19

According to the scriptures, the Jews had asked Jesus for a sign to show his authority. When Jesus answered them by saying, "if you destroy this temple, I will build it up in three days," they were livid. According to the text, "It has taken Forty- six years to build this temple and you are going to build it up in three days" (John 2:20).

This shows that the Jews were not connected in the spirit realm, so they could not understand what Jesus was saying. Many times we see or feel God moving in a particular way, and because it deviates from the "norm," we are unable to understand it. As a result, we tend to make all kinds of negative remarks. The term "eternal" is used to describe God, which means that he is not limited by time or space, but that he has no beginning or end (Towns, 2008). Furthermore, Jesus Christ is a part of the "Trinity," meaning that he is one with God, the Father, and the Holy Spirit. Therefore, we have to worship him in the Spirit. "God is a spirit and they that worship Him must worship Him is spirit and in truth" (John 4:24).

TAKING ON THE APPEARANCE OF CHRIST

Think about when a woman is pregnant; that child grows in the womb for nine months. At the end of the ninth months, the child is mature and ready to be born. When the child is born, in most cases, he is immediately introduced to the mother's breast. From there he connects with the mother and becomes sensitized to the smell and warmth of the mother, and those around him. As he matures he begins to demonstrate certain traits that we can ascribe to the mother, the father, or other members of the family. And when he is old enough, he may look just like his mother or father or some other member of the family. In the same way, when we are born of the Spirit, we are brought to full maturity by meditating on the word. As we begin to drink the word, feast on the word, and meditate on the Word of God, we become mature and ready to go to the next level in Christ. Additionally, we begin to look more and more like Christ in our thought process, our actions, and our appearance. We begin to understand more about the things of the Spirit as we die to the flesh. I firmly hold to the view that Christ did not only come to die for our sins and to teach, preach, and perform miracles, but I believe that he came to show us how to live in the Spirit while we are yet in the flesh. According to 1 Corinthians 2:14, "But the natural man does not receive the things of the Spirit of God, for they are foolish to him; nor can he know them, because they are spiritually discerned." Therefore, for us to understand the things of the Spirit, we have to walk in the Spirit, because the things of God are caught, not taught.

REFLECTION

The story is told of Nicodemus who came to Jesus by night. When Jesus told him that he must be born again in order to enter the kingdom of heaven. Nicodemus was baffled. He asked Jesus, "Can a man be born when he is old? Can he enter a second time into his mother's womb" (John 3:1-21) You see Jesus was talking about matter pertaining to the spirit not the flesh. How many times have we missed what God was saying or doing because we were walking in the flesh?

ACTIVITY
STOP-AND-THINK

CONSIDER THE QUOTE

The Spirit of the Lord is like the stars that illuminates my soul.

Who can control it, sustain it, or detain it.

The spirit of the Lord is like fire shut up in my bones.

Let's just perceive it, maintain it, and proclaim it (Latoya Panton)

1. What are two words that come to mind when you think of the Spirit of God?
2. Why does Christ encourages us to walk in the spirit?

WHO AM I IN GOD

When I am connected to God, I am a mighty force;
I am an eagle not a weasel, or a beetle.
When I am connected to God, I am
a mighty army, a fire carrier.
I am a mighty force, not a curse, nor am I the worst.
When I am connected to God, I am a survivor
More than a conqueror, I am a warrior.
---Latoya Panton

CHAPTER 7

USING THE WEAPON OF PRAYER

E ver encountered something so powerful that it could transform a negative situation into a positive one or make a dead situation come alive within a split second? Well, prayer was my answer. "Prayer is a two-way communication tool between man and God, a two-way relationship in which man should not only talk to God, but also listen to Him" (Billy Graham).

The Word of God admonishes us to pray always. "Praying always with all prayer, and supplication in the Spirit; and watching there unto with all perseverance and supplication for all saints" (Ephesians 6:18). "Call unto me, and I will answer thee, and shew thee great and mighty things, which thou knowest not" (Jeremiah 33:3). Like fuel provides the energy that allows the car to operate, prayer provides the energy we need to live an effective Christian life in God. There are many kinds of prayer to combat the different situations in our life. There are prayers of repentance, prayers of intercession, prophetic prayers, warfare prayers, and prayers of thanksgiving, healing, and deliverance and so on. Luke 21:35 states, "Watch therefore, and pray always that you may be counted worthy to escape all these things that will come to pass and to stand before the son of man." In the book of Luke, we see where Jesus was teaching about the end times and encouraging the people to watch and pray so that they may be found worthy to stand before the son of man. So while we pray for the things we need, and we pray for others, we should also pray to escape the wrath that is to come and to stand before God.

REFLECTION

A day without prayer is a day without blessing, and life without prayer is a life without power (Edwin Harvey). How is this statement true?

One of the most powerful prayers that I saw in the Bible was the prayer of Hezekiah. Here was Hezekiah, a man of God who had upheld the principles and precepts of God. In fact, Hezekiah was responsible for rebuilding the temple of worship in his time. He sought to do what was just and honorable before God. However, he was soon given the most horrific news that would change his life within a split second. Isaiah was sent by God to warn him to put his house in order and to get ready to die. Upon hearing the news; Hezekiah did not show any signs of emotional weakness in the presence of the prophet of God but received the word and waited for Isaiah to leave before going to God and reminding him of his faithfulness to him. According to 2 Kings 20:2–3, "Then he turned his face toward the wall and prayed to the Lord, saying Remember now, O Lord, I pray, how I have walked before You in truth and with a loyal heart, and have done what was good in Your sight, And Hezekiah wept bitterly." This not only showed the spiritual authority that Hezekiah had but showed that Hezekiah had a deep relationship with God and knew that through prayer he could touch God. Today we can touch God through prayer. The ability for God to answer and deliver is not dependent on how grave the situation may look, but it is dependent on our faith in him. His word declares that we are justified by faith (Romans 5:1) and that faith without works is dead (James 2:14–26).

WHY WARFARE PRAYERS?

"Though we walk in the flesh we do not war according to the flesh, for the weapons of our warfare are not carnal but are mighty in the pulling down of stronghold" (2 Corinthians 10:3–6). This scripture suggest that not only are we in a war, but we also are in spiritual warfare. This war that we fight is not fought with machine guns and cannons, but with the spiritual missiles of the word and the power of God. Hence, the scripture encourages us to put on the whole armor of God that we may be able the withstand the fiery darts of the enemy.

Ephesians 6:11–18, King James Version (KJV):

Put on the whole armor of God, that ye may be able to stand against the wiles of the devil. For we wrestle not against flesh and blood, but against principalities, against powers, against the rulers of the darkness of this world, against spiritual wickedness in high places.

Hence, this scripture supports the idea that principalities and powers are real and not just a fictitious thought. The word "principality" refers to a position of authority held by a prince: "(1) The state, office, or authority of a prince, the position or responsibilities of a principal (as of a school) or (2) the territory or jurisdiction of a prince: the country that gives title to a prince" (*Merriam-Webster's*). The story is told in the Bible of Daniel, who after receiving a troubling vision concerning a great war, started a period of a twenty-one-day prayer and fasting. Immediately, God heard his prayer and sent an angel with the explanation of the dream. But on his way to Daniel, the angel was withstood for the same amount of time by the prince of Persia.

Later, Michael, one of the chief angels, had to come and free him from the clutches of the demonic angel that had held him captive. The angel further went on to anticipate another encounter with the prince of Greece (Daniel 10). This passage of scripture further supports the need for us to be aware of the unforeseen forces that we fight. Hence, if we do not know what we are fighting against, we will not be able to fight effectively.

REFLECTION

"Be alert and of sober mind, Your enemy the devil prowls around like a roaring lion looking for someone to devour" (1 Peter 5: 8).

This scripture suggest that we are fighting against the devil. As a result, we need to equip ourselves with the right spiritual tools. What are some spiritual tools that you have in your arsenal to fight against the wiles of the devil?

DEALING WITH THE SPIRIT OF OPPRESSION

Oftentimes we find ourselves being oppressed, or suppressed, in one form or another. Whether it be social oppression, interpersonal suppression, or systematic suppression, we are impacted in some way or another. Oppression is a system that maintains advantage and disadvantage based on social group memberships and operates, intentionally and unintentionally, on individual, institutional, and cultural levels (Gender Power and Privilege Blog). According to *Merriam-Webster's Dictionary*, "Oppression is the unjust or cruel exercise of authority." The effects of oppression continue to wreak havoc in our society today. The people of Israel experienced many different forms of oppression at the harsh hands of the Egyptians. The Israelites sojourned in the land of Egypt for 430 years. However, during the course of time when the Pharaoh realized that they had become numerous, he became fearful that they would come together and turn against him. Subsequently, he ordered the killing of the male children and increased the workload of the Israelites, forcing them to produce more work within a shorter time frame. The Pharaoh placed taskmasters over them and ordered them to find their own straw to make bricks and to produce the same amount of bricks in the same time frame. This strategy had all the ingredients of oppression. It was bad enough that they had to find their own straw to make bricks and did not get extended time to produce the work, but to also order the midwives to not help the women when they were on the birthing table was like rubbing salt into a wound. Furthermore, when they did give birth to their babies, the Pharaoh ordered them to be killed or thrown into the Nile. The Israelites were experiencing large-scale oppression. They were not just oppressed institutionally/systematically, but they were also oppressed socially, emotionally, physically, and mentally. In our current world, this same thread of oppression runs deep within the fabric of our society. A Linder study (as cited in Linder et. al, 2019) states, "Oppression often pits people with minoritized identity against each other, clamoring against the same semblance of power." In this chapter, I will look at three levels of oppression: individual oppression, institutional oppression, and societal/cultural oppression.

Individual Oppression: Attitudes and actions that reflect prejudice against a social group (intentional and unintentional).

Institutional Oppression: Policies, laws, rules, norms, and customs enacted by organizations and social institutions that disadvantage some social groups and advantage other social groups. These institutions include religion, the government, education, law, the media, and the health-care system (intentional and unintentional).

Societal/Cultural Oppression: Social norms, roles, rituals, language, music, and art that reflect and reinforce the belief that one social group is superior to another (intentional and unintentional).

Hence, in order for us to effectively stand against these different forms of oppression, and other unseen spiritual forces, we have to employ the weapon of prayer. Prayer is the spiritual weapon that God has given each and every one of us to pull down principalities and powers and spiritual wickedness in high places. Furthermore, God gives his perspective on oppression in his word. The book of Luke 4:18–19 states, "The Spirit of the Lord is upon me, because he has anointed me to proclaim good news to the poor. He has sent me to proclaim liberty to the captives and recovering of sight to the blind, to set at liberty those who are oppressed, to proclaim the year of the Lord's favor."

Spiritual Warfare Prayers against the Plans of the Enemy

Scripture Reading: Psalms 25

Warfare Scripture: Psalms 35:1–3 states, "Plead my cause, O Lord, with them that strive with me: fight against them that fight against me. Take hold of shield and buckler, and stand up for mine help. Draw out also the spear, and stop the way against them that persecute me: say unto my soul, I am thy salvation."

- By the power that sank the Pharaoh, let my stubborn problems die in the name of Jesus.
- By the power that disgraced Goliath, let my stubborn problems die in the name of Jesus.
- Holy Ghost, fire arise and attack my mountain in the name of Jesus.
- Every witchcraft incantation against my destiny, die in the name of Jesus.
- Every trouble of the night, die in the name of Jesus.

- Every power of the enemy, catch the fire of the almighty God in the name of Jesus.
- Every arrow that flies by day and by night attacking my star, die in the name of Jesus.
- Spirit of the living God, pursue my stubborn pursuers in the name of Jesus.
- Every mocking yoke in my life, die in the name of Jesus.
- Let the God of Elijah that answers by fire send fire upon my enemies in the name of Jesus.
- Evil pursuers parading on my terrain catch the fire of the living God in the name of Jesus.
- Every demonic agenda of the enemy orchestrated against my life, die in the name of Jesus.
- Almighty God who is the head of all principalities and powers, disarm every principality and power in the name of Jesus.

REFLECTION

The word of God admonishes us to put on the spiritual armor of salvation. What are some of the spiritual covering that we need to put on as we combat the enemies plans?

DECLARATIVE PRAYERS

*Prayer of declaration simply means that once we
know God's heart on an issue, we boldly pray
that it will be so, and then walk in faith that it is
already so—even if the answer is not yet visible.*
—Jonathan Graf

Declarative prayers are prayers of authority and faith knowing that whatever you ask in the name of Jesus, it shall be granted. In Genesis we see where God said, Let there be light, and there was light (Genesis 1:3). God demonstrated his very authority of creation by speaking a word into existence. In the beginning God created heaven and the earth. And God said, Let there be light: and there was light. And God saw the light, that it was good: and God divided the light from the darkness. And God called the light Day, and the darkness he called Night (Genesis 1:1–3). After rereading chapter one of Genesis, I am more convinced than ever that whatever we want to happen in our lives, we have to declare it in faith. God through his infinite wisdom and knowledge laid the example for us when he spoke the world into being. As a result, he has given us the spiritual authority to declare his word over our lives and allow him to do the rest.

Jeremiah 1:10 states, "See, I have this day set you over the nations and over the kingdom. To root out and to pull down, To destroy and to throw down, To build and to plant." Hence, it is incumbent upon us to utilize the Word of God to our full capacity over our lives and over difficult situations so that we will be able to walk in victory.

PERSONAL DECLARATIVE PRAYERS

Scripture Reading: Ephesians 1:17–23 states, "That the God of our Lord Jesus Christ, the Father of glory, may give to you the spirit of wisdom and revelation in the knowledge of Him."

Declarative Scripture: Psalms 91

- Covenant keeping God of the nations of the earth, there is none like you.
- You reign and rule from generation to generation.
- Your name is exalted forever, and your name and is above every other name
- We decree and declare that like Jebez you will enlarge our territories and that you will bless us indeed in the name of Jesus.
- We decree and declare that as the mountains surround Jerusalem, that you will surround us in the mighty name of Jesus.
- We decree and declare that as you part the Red Sea for the people of Israel that you will part the red sea for us in the mighty name of Jesus.

- We declare that we will walk in our destiny and spiritual fulfillment in the name of Jesus.
- We decree and declare that as we live in a time of fulfillment of your word, that we will catch a spiritual revelation of you in the name of Jesus.
- We decree and declare that as we live in a time of the prophetic fulfillment, we pray that an overflow of the prophetic dispensation of your anointing will be released upon us in the name of Jesus.
- We pray that you will equip us with the spiritual frontline battle armor to fight the giants of oppression in our time in the name of Jesus.
- We pray that your spiritual army will rise in alignment from the east coast to the west coast in the mighty name of Jesus.
- We decree and declare that the sons of men in our nation will rise up in power and authority in the mighty name of Jesus.
- We decree and declare that we will catch a spiritual revelation of what you are doing in this time and align ourselves with your word in the mighty name of Jesus.
- We decree and declare that every department of justice in this nation will rise up with holy indignation against the spirit of injustice in the name of Jesus.
- We decree and declare that the cry for justice from our lips will saturate the atmosphere and

that the angel of mercy and peace will comfort the souls of men in the name of Jesus.

REFLECTION

What are some things that you are declaring for God to do over your life and the lives of your family?

Prayer of Intercession

According to Widmer (2014), "Intercessory prayer is basically petitionary prayer that is brought before God on behalf of someone else." In 1 Timothy 2:5, Jesus is not only seen as our intercessor, but also our mediator: "For there is one God and one mediator between God and mankind, the man Christ Jesus." The scripture speaks of many different forms of intercessions. Some of these include nation, mercy, and worship intercessions. In the book of Exodus, we saw where Moses pleaded for God to have mercy on the people of Israel (Exodus 32:11–13). "Then Moses pleaded with the Lord his God, and said: 'Lord, why does Your wrath burn hot against Your people whom You have brought out of the land of Egypt with great power and with a mighty hand?' Why should the Egyptians speak, and say, 'He brought them out to harm them, to kill them in the mountains, and to consume them from the face of the earth'? Turn from Your fierce wrath, and relent from this harm to Your people. Remember Abraham, Isaac, and Israel, Your servants, to whom You swore by Your own self, and said to them, 'I will multiply your descendants as the stars of heaven; and all this land that I have spoken of I give to your descendants, and they shall inherit *it* forever.'" Here we see Moses assuming the role of an intercessor, pleading with God on the behalf of the children of Israel and reminding God of his covenant with Abraham, Isaac, and Jacob. Later we saw where God relented from harming the people of Israel (Exodus 32:14). The Word of God admonishes us to come boldly before the throne of grace to obtain mercy and find grace from God to help us through difficult situations. "Let us therefore come boldly unto the throne of grace, that we may obtain mercy, and find grace to help in time of need" (Hebrews 4:16).

REFLECTION

What is your petition to God for your family, for you school, and for your country?

INTERCESSION FOR THE NATION—HAVE MERCY UPON YOUR PEOPLE, OH GOD

Scripture Reading: Psalms 27:9 states, "Do not hide Your face from me; Do not turn Your servant away in anger; You have been my help; Do not leave me nor forsake me, O God of my salvation."

Confession: "Out of the depths I cry to you, O Lord. Lord, hear my voice! Let your ears be attentive to the voice of my supplications! If you, O Lord, should mark iniquities, Lord, who could stand? But there is forgiveness with you that you may be feared" (Psalm 130:1–4).

- Covenant-keeping God of the nations of the earth, there is none like you who forgives the sins of men.
- Oh God, you reign and rule from generation to generation.
- Father Lord, your people have acknowledged their transgressions before you and ask that you pardon their sins in the name of Jesus.

- Father, Lord, we pray that you will not punish your people as their sins deserve, but that you will temper judgment with mercy in the mighty name of Jesus.

- Father, Lord, seventy times seven you have forgiven your people, oh Lord, but they keep sinning against you, oh Lord.

- Father, Lord, we pray that you will forgive your people and help them to find grace to walk in righteousness in the name of Jesus.

- Father, Lord, we pray that though our sins are like scarlet, you will make them as white as snow in the name of Jesus.

- Father, Lord, we pray that you will restore the joy of your people to its former glory in the name of Jesus.

- Father, Lord, we pray that you will restore the integrity of your people in the name of Jesus.

- Father, Lord, we pray that you will reign down compassion on your people once again.

- Almighty God, we pray that as the heavens are higher than the earth, so will the sins of your people be far from you in the name of Jesus.

- Almighty Father, we pray that you will cast the sins of your people into the sea of forgetfulness in the name of Jesus.

- The I AM That I AM, we pray that you will restore to your people the years that the locust has eaten and the years that the cankerworm has eaten, in the name of Jesus.

- Father, Lord, we pray that you will remove the spirit of infirmities from your people in the name of Jesus.

- Father, Lord, we pray that you will remove the plagues and pestilence from among your people in the name of Jesus.

- Jehovah Jireh, we pray that you will send divine healing and restoration to your people in the name of Jesus.

- Father, Lord, we pray that you will help your people to walk in alignment to your word in the name of Jesus. Amen.

ACTIVITY
STOP-AND PRAY

REFLECTION
In the bible we see where Daniel prayed three times a day. (Daniel 6:10) What is your prayer challenge?

CHAPTER 8

PRAISE THAT UNLOCKS
HEAVEN'S PORTAL

Have you ever been in a situation where you felt like you had met your end; or lost everything and then like the phoenix from the ashes your rose stronger, smarter or more powerful? Well, that was me in my "Marah" situation. My ability to praise God through difficult situations changed my outcome from dwindling in defeat, to fulfilling God's purpose in my life.

PRAISING YOUR WAY OUT

In education "praise" refers to, "positive evaluation made by a person of another's' products, performance or attributes where the evaluator presumes the validity of the standards on which the evaluation is based" (Henderlong & Lepper, 2002). Hence praise is a very important aspect of the teaching and learning environment. If you want a child to do well you must first identify areas of strengths within that child and consistently nurture those strengths with praises and affirmations to ensure continued growth, and success. In the same way, if we want to unlock the blessings of God, we need to adopt the weapon of praise. Like education is the key to unlock any door. Praise is the key to unlock heaven's portal. Furthermore, if you ever wondered, "How do I get close to God? Well, praise would be your answer. "Praise the LORD, O servants of the LORD, praise the name of the LORD" (Psalms 113:1).While at the backside of the dessert I was able to top into a reservoir of praise that I didn't even know existed. Every time the enemy would shoot out his poisonous venom at me I would serve up an entree of praise to God. Which eventually broke out into worship, and prayer. Here my spiritual muscles of praise and worship would rise to another level. And though I was still confronted by the enemy I was in a place of spiritual power to attack him head on.

PRAISE IS WHAT WE DO

The story is told in the bible of how David worshiped the Lord after he had brought back the Ark of God from the house of Obed-edom to the city of David. And it was told to King David,

"The Lord has blessed the household of Obed-edom and all that belongs to him, because of the ark of God."

So David went and brought up the ark of God from the house of Obed-edom to the city of David with rejoicing; and when those who bore the ark of the Lord had gone six steps, he sacrificed an ox and a fattened animal. And David danced before the Lord with all his might; and David was wearing a linen ephod" (2 Samuel 6:12-14). Here we see David offering up burnt offering to God and dancing before the Lord. Like David we should praise the God for what he has done in our lives. Praise him for delivering us out of the evil clutch of the enemy. Praise him in dance; praise him with the timbrels' praise him with the drums; praise him with joyful shouts of praise. Psalms 150:1-6, "Praise ye the LORD. Praise God in his sanctuary: praise him in the firmament of his power. Praise him for his mighty acts: praise him according to his excellent greatness. Praise him with the sound of the trumpet: praise him with the psaltery and harp. Praise him with the timbrel and dance: praise him with stringed instruments and organs. Praise him upon the loud cymbals: praise him upon the high sounding cymbals. Let everything that hath breath praise the LORD. Praise ye the LORD."

YOU WILL BE HATED FOR YOUR PRAISE

We see in the scriptures that when David had brought back the Ark to the city of David that his wife Michal looked at him with contempt. "But as the Ark of the LORD entered the City of David, Michal, the daughter of Saul, looked down from her window. When she saw King David leaping and dancing before the LORD, she was filled with contempt for him." (2 Samuel 6:16) David later rebuked Michal and in the final verse we see that Michal had no children. Many people believed that this was Michal's punishment for looking at her husband's act of worship to God with abhorrence. Other's believed that David refused to have any sexual relationship with her, and thus she did not have any children. Whatever, the case, David acts of worship to God should never have been questioned, because God had delivered him out of the hands of his enemies numerous times; so, it was only appropriate for David to praise God the way he did.

Like Michal, many people will not understand your praise. But, I have come to understand that people will not understand your praise until they understand what God has done for you. I remember in 2018, I had a terrible car accident, where my car was totaled, but God brought me out without a catch. I remember sitting in the driver's seat and hearing the liquid running from the radiator and thinking that I could not have possibly survived this. Later, I would find myself coming out of the vehicle with no major injuries. Today, I praise God because of who he is and for what he has done for me. I have come to know him as a very present help in the time of trouble. I have come to know him as my refuge and my fortress; my strong tower.

REFLECTION

I have often heard many testimonials from people where God had delivered them from crack cocaine, or delivered them from being killed by their pursuers. What is one thing that God delivered you from, that you knew it had to be God?

PRAISE GOD IN WHATEVER SITUATION YOU FIND YOURSELF IN

"Some people complain because God puts thorns on roses, while others praise him for putting roses among thorns."
--Unknown

Understanding that God is God no matter the circumstances; will help us to praise him despite what we go through. God in his nature is, Spirit, life, self-existent, unchanging, unlimited by time and space (Elmer Towns, 2008). God is described in Revelation as the Alpha and the Omega, the first and the last, the beginning and the end. (Revelation 22: 13)

If there was ever a man who knew how to praise God despite his circumstances, it would be Job. As we know it, Job was an upstanding man in the land of Uz. The Word of God said, he was blameless and upright; and that he feared

God and shunned evil. (Job 1:1) But as time went by, Job would lose all his possessions, his wealth and his children in one day. (Job 1:13-18) At this point, I think it would be perfectly understandable if Job decided to go on a rampage, sip on a bottle of whisky, and shaved the hair off his head. Well, he actually did, but instead of cursing God, and getting all crazy; he decided to worship God. (Job 1:20-22) As I go through my own struggles; and experienced some really trying situations; I know that it takes the mercies and grace on one's life to get to a place where you praise God despite the storms that one experiences. Our ability to "put a praise on it" even when the situation looks grave, or deleterious will determine our outcome both spiritually, and physically.

REFLECTION

Have you ever had a Job experience? What was your initial reaction?

TEN REASONS WHY WE SHOULD PRAISE GOD

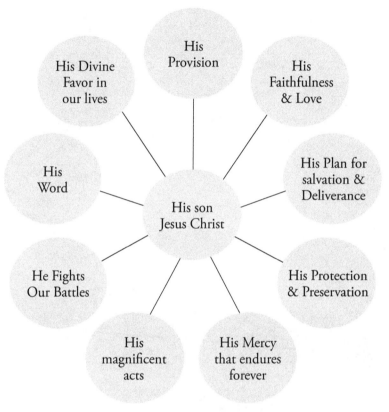

ACTIVITY
STOP-AND-THINK

What are three reasons why you praise God?

1. _____

2. _____

3. _____

CONCLUSION

In essence, I have come to understand that God's purpose and prophecy in our lives does not change simply because we change locations, or become older. God told Jeremiah, "Before I formed you in the womb I knew you; I sanctified you; I ordained you a prophet to the nations" (Jeremiah 1:5). The act of God working and fulfilling his missions in our lives does not depend on our feelings. Whether we think we are good enough or not good enough. Five years ago when I was asked to pray at a crusade at my local church, I remember asking God what to pray about. That morning he told me to remind the people in prayer that "He is not like the weather; he does not change. He is not like the dollar; he does not devalue. And he is not like man; he is not stirred by emotions." Hence, God is eternal. He does not change. He is the word. He is the door. He is the Lamb of God that sits on the throne. He is infinite, meaning he is unlimited, unrestricted, and all powerful.

Walking in the Prophetic Anointing will also serve to keep us focus on the call and purpose of God on our lives.

Living a life of constant prayer will help us to stay connected to God, and to hear his voice. For me, Walking in the Prophetic Anointing has helped me to overcome the many battles, and lies of the enemy, and to carry out the mission and purpose of God in my life.

References

Broun, K. S. (2012). Saving nelson mandela : The rivonia trial and the fate of south africa. Retrieved from https://ebookcentral-proquest-com.library.capella.edu

Carpendale, J. I. M., & Müller, U. (Eds.). (2003). Social interaction and the development of knowledge. Retrieved from https://ebookcentral-proquest-com.library.capella.edu

Deal, T. E., & Peterson, K. D. (2016). Shaping school culture. Retrieved from https://ebookcentral-proquest-com.library.capella.edu

East, J. F. (2018). Transformational leadership for the helping professions : Engaging head, heart, and soul. Retrieved from https://ebookcentral-proquest-com.library.capella.edu

Hildrew, C. (2018). Becoming a growth mindset school: The power of mindset to transform teaching, leadership and learning. Retrieved from https://ebookcentral-proquest-com.library.capella.edu

https://www.biblegateway.com/versions/New-King-James-Version-NKJV-Bible/

https://digitalcommons.georgefox.edu/cgi/viewcontent.cgi?article=1139&context=wes_theses

https://www.reed.edu/motivation/docs/PraiseReview.pdf

http://www.intercessorsarise.org/declarative-prayer

https://www.kingjamesbibleonline.org/Genesis-1-3/

http://ws405.blogspot.com/2011/01/understanding-oppression.html

https://d1wqtxts1xzle7.cloudfront.net/30661094/thepsychologist_
0104furn.pdf?1361908427=&response-content-disposition
=inline%3B+filename%3DEducation_and_culture_shock.
pdf&Expires

Linder, C., Quaye, S. J., Lange, A. C., Evans, M. E., & Stewart, T. J.
(2019). Identity-based student activism: Power and oppression
on college campuses. Retrieved from https://ebookcentral-
proquest-com.library.capella.edu

Madsen, J. A., & Mabokela, R. O. (2005). Culturally relevant schools
: Creating positive workplace relationships and preventing
intergroup differences. Retrieved from https://ebookcentral-
proquest-com.library.capella.edu

Neumann, K. L., & Kopcha, T. J. (2018). The Use of Schema Theory
in Learning, Design, and Technology. TechTrends: Linking
Research & Practice to Improve Learning, 62(5), 429–431.
https://doi.org/10.1007/s11528-018-0319-0

Towns, E. (2008.) Theology for Today:

Widmer, M. (2014). Standing in the breach: An old testament
theology and spirituality of intercessory prayer. Retrieved from
https://ebookcentral-proquest-com.library.capella.edu

Appendix 1
Terms and Definitions

Affirmations: An act of saying or showing that something is true (*Merriam-Webster's*). Why affirm? These are useful tools for trying to cultivate the atmosphere or the dreams that you have planned for yourself. In my personal experiences, I have had to affirm myself of who I was and what I wanted to become despite how the situations around me appeared.

Culture Shock: In Oberg study (as cited by Adrian Furnham) is defined as a strain due to the effort required to make necessary psychological adaptations; a sense of loss and feelings of deprivation in regard to friends, status, profession and possessions; being rejected by, or rejecting, members of the new culture; confusion in role, role expectations, values; surprise, anxiety, even disgust and indignation after becoming aware of cultural differences; feelings of impotence due to not being able to cope with the new environment.

Mindset: Having the right mindset can determine whether you fail or succeed at something. Hence, it is important that we constantly check our mindset when we are faced with a new challenge or placed in an unfamiliar situation. Mindset is defined as a mental attitude or inclination (*Merriam-Webster's Dictionary*).

Fixed Mindset: People with a fixed mindset are those who are limited by what they think they can do. Most times these are people who see other people as more capable or better than themselves. According to Hildrew (2018), "In the fixed mindset you believe that your qualities are carved in stone."

Growth Mindset: People with a growth mindset see challenges, obstacles, and failures as opportunities to rise, try again, and improve their skills, knowledge, and abilities. In this mindset you believe that the abilities and qualities you are born with can be developed and cultivated through efforts, application, experience, and practice (Hildrew, 2018).

APPENDIX 2
WARFARE SCRIPTURES

EPHESIANS 6:12–13

12 For we do not wrestle against flesh and blood, but against principalities, against powers, against the rulers of [a]the darkness of this age, against spiritual *hosts* of wickedness in the heavenly *places*. 13 Therefore take up the whole armor of God, that you may be able to withstand in the evil day, and having done all, to stand.

PSALM 144:1

Praise be to the *LORD* *my* Rock, who trains *my hands* for *war, my fingers* for *battle.* He is *my* loving *God* and *my* fortress, *my* stronghold and *my* deliverer, *my* shield, in whom I take refuge, who subdues peoples under me.

PSALMS 35:1–2

1 Plead my cause, O Lord, with them that strive with me: fight against them that fight against me.
2 Take hold of shield and buckler, and stand up for mine help

PSALMS 35:4

4 Let them be confused and put to shame that seek after my soul: let them be turned back and brought to confusion that devises my hurt.

ISAIAH 54:16–17

"Behold, I have created the blacksmith
Who blows the coals in the fire,
Who brings forth an [a] instrument for his work;
And I have created the [b] spoiler to destroy.

No weapon formed against you shall prosper,
And every tongue which rises against you in judgment
You shall condemn.
This is the heritage of the servants of the Lord,
And their righteousness is from Me,"
Says the Lord.

PSALM 91:

1 He who dwells in the secret place of the Most High will rest in the shadow of the Almighty.
2 I will say of Yahweh, "He is my refuge and my fortress; my God, in whom I trust."

APPENDIX 3
SPIRITUAL AFFIRMATIONS

- When I pass through unfamiliar waters, I will be still and know that God is God.
- When the cares of life seem to overwhelm me, the Lord will be my exceedingly great reward.
- When I am in distress, I will run to the rock that is higher than I am.
- When the enemy tries to buffet me, I will call upon the God that strengthens the weak with his salvation.
- When darkness tries to overpower me, I will seek the true light that shines in the darkness.
- When my joy is fulfilled, I will sing praises to the God who is eternal and immortal, the only wise God.
- When I am faced with insecurities, I will remember that I am complete, I am whole, and I am lacking nothing.
- Because he purchased my salvation, I will enjoy the goodness of the Lord in the land of the living.
- I am the apple of God's eye; therefore, he will perfect that which concerns me.
- By the same power that raised Lazarus from the dead, I will pull down strongholds in my life.
- When I pass through the waters, I will not drown. When I pass through the floods, it will not overwhelm me. When I pass through the fire, I will not be burned.

ABOUT THE AUTHOR

Latoya Hewitt Panton is an educator who hails from the beautiful island of Jamaica. Latoya has served in the field of education for over seventeen years. She has taught at various grade levels ranging for second through to seventh. She has a passion for God and enjoys teaching and inspiring others in the faith. She is the only child to Zichar Kathleen Morrison, and the wife of seventeen years to Ernesto Panton. She has two boys who serve to inspire her.

Her goal is to continue to fulfill God's purpose in her life, and to inspire, and empower others. Latoya also supports numerous charity foundations around the world and hopes to continue to impact the lives of others positively.